Extreme Overflow Publishing
Dacula, GA
USA

© Copyright 2021 Ralph W. Diggs

All rights reserved. No part of this book may be reproduced or transmitted in any form or by any means electronic or mechanical photocopying, recording or by any information storage and retrieval system without the prior written permission of the author, except for the inclusion of brief quotations in critical reviews and certain other noncommercial uses permitted by copyright law. For permission requests, contact the publisher.

Extreme Overflow Publishing
Dacula, GA
USA

Extreme Overflow Publishing
A Brand of Extreme Overflow Enterprises, Inc
P.O. Box 1811
Dacula, GA 30019

www.extremeoverflow.com
Send feedback to info@extremeoverflow.com

Printed in the United States of America

Library of Congress Catalogin-Publication
Data is available for this title. ISBN: 978-1-7351257-6-3

THE CHEAT CODE

A Fundamental Guide to Financial Freedom

Ralph W. Diggs

Table of Contents

Introduction 6

Humble Beginnings: My Background Story 10

Basic Investing 30

Assets in Your portfolio; Why Do They Matter? 84

Time Management and Productivity Hacks 101

Creating a Business or Investing in Your Niche:
Which is Better for You? 110

Budgeting for Your Business Goals 121

CEO Mind-Set 129

Retirement Investing for Generational Wealth 136

The Evolution of An Investor 140

Introduction

If you're holding this book right now, chances are you have a lot of questions about money.

Have you ever wondered why some people seem to be financially free and in control of their wealth throughout their lives, and you're not? Have you ever wondered: how do they do it? How do they get to predict the financial aspect of their lives with so much certainty, and have what they predicted come through for them? How do they get to leave an amazing legacy for their children, and see them grow into privileged lives, with a lot of benefits and good things happening for them?

How?

Is there an unfair thread that holds everything in this world at a place where they are without the control of man? Or are these people just plain lucky, as they would most likely want you to believe? You might even be looking at the people who are dangling off the bottom of the other end of the chain and can't help the feeling of anxiety that springs up within you.

These are the ones who cannot afford any luxury in life, or they cannot afford a lot of the luxuries they would want to have in their lives. They would like to sit back and travel the world and be able to treat themselves and the people around them to the good things of life, but they are sadly incapacitated in this way.

Sometimes, they troll the streets all day looking for any means of help and seeking to find if there is any stroke of luck that will shine down on them for a day. They are the ones that people hardly ever want to mingle with, hardly want to be associated with; and they are the ones whom people think cannot amount to much in the grand scheme of things. If you have felt any variant of the thoughts above, chances are you are reading the right book.

At this point, you might be wondering:

- How do I step out of the shadows of lack and poverty and into the light that comes with the knowledge that I am free from worrying about money and financial constraints in life?

- How do I get the life I so desire and deserve for myself and for the people that matter in my life?

- How do I multiply my money so that I can have

- enough for myself, and I am in a position to lay up wealth for my children and their children so that they have a healthy head start in their lives?

I can feel the wheels in your mind turning right now. If you have found yourself asking any of these questions, then congratulations are in order.

Congratulations!

You deserve to be congratulated for taking a step to ensure that you step out of poverty and a life of lack and into the life you were designed for; and called to live – that is the life of abundance.

Congratulations on deciding to put your best foot forward and deciding to go for the best, and deciding to bridge the gap that has existed for a long time in your life and in the lives of the people you love.

In this book, you will be exposed to tips and proven strategies to get you out of the lower class of earners and into the class of the elite. If you use this cheat code with an open heart and with the intention to learn and apply what you have learned, you will see the change and live big results in your life.

Why am I sure of what I am telling you?

I am certain because these are the strategies I used to achieve the finical success I have today. With the strategies you will learn in this book, you will step up your life and set up your life for financial freedom. Also, these same strategies have worked for countless other people I know over time.

The truth is this book you're holding is much more than a book. It is a template that will help you gain financial freedom and set you on track to achieving the financial aims you have set for yourself. This way, you can get a shot at finally living the life you desire, the life of financial freedom.

So, are you ready to take charge of your finances?

If so, continue reading.

If not, still keep reading.

… your life is about to be transformed.

1

HUMBLE BEGINNINGS: MY BACKGROUND STORY

Today is the first day of the rest of your life. And no, this is not a curse.

By picking up this book you are holding in your hand right now, you have made a great decision; and you are on the right track to revamping your financial status and making the most out of the rest of your life – in terms of money.

Before we get ahead of ourselves, let me tell you a little story. Growing up in a tough neighborhood, the people we looked up to weren't always the best option. The things they had made them hard to miss. As kids, we wondered how they had the cars and clothes. The older we got, we started to understand how they did it; and we knew it wasn't fully legit but understood they need to make a living, so we just watched in awe. I told myself I would be smarter with money when I got older and not be so flashy like the corner fellas.

If you're like me, the thought of gaining financial freedom seemed to be a herculean task that only a handful of people actually got to achieve. None of them I knew. In my world, if you were ever rich, one of two things must have happened.

A. You either worked three jobs at the same time...

The funny part was that working more jobs never actually got anyone I knew to become rich, although it came in handy if you were looking for a way to clear your debts in a get-so-stressed-until-you-forget-your-name way.

Or...

B. You won the lottery.

Not a lot of people I saw who won the lottery actually retained their wealth. One day they were filthy rich and could afford to do and spend anything. The next day they were back at square zero with nothing to show for it.

It was as though the world was sitting precariously on a ledge, and notwithstanding what happened, something was going to take place to counteract the effect of any good stroke of luck that shone down on people.

The thing was that for a long time, there seemed to be this ledge that existed for the sole purpose of separating the really rich people from those who were not at their level in the society. So, there was a major disconnect between the rich, the well-to-do, and the poor.

Don't even get me started on talking about what it felt like to be a part of the population of poor people. It was a terrible experience, to be frank.

Having to stare longingly at the finest of silk materials that gleamed in the evening sunlight as the rich stepped out of their vintage cars with huge, "perfect" smiles on their faces and exchanged pleasantries with themselves was a difficult thing. Just breathing in and holding your breath for much longer so that by any chance, you could get a whiff of their expensive cologne as it wrapped around their bodies in a gentle grip was how we did it, at first.

That was me, a few years back.

I was not what I considered to be rich.

I was considered a healthy child when I was born on

September 9th, at Brigham and Women's Hospital in Boston, Massachusetts. My mom, Antinette Houston, was married to my dad, Ralph W. Diggs Jr, and at the time of my birth they did not have a lot. During my early days at home, we made do with a lot of hand me down clothes, and we had to find creative ways to cut costs for just about everything you could possibly think of.

I remember all the times I had to stare at the screen of the television in longing as I saw all the pictures and videos of the people who were privileged in life. I just did not understand what it felt like to be privileged, as it was not yet a possibility to me and the members of my family. Inasmuch as my parents seemed to be content with the lives we had, and we could barely scrape it through every day; I knew there could be more and that there were possibilities of breaking out of the shell of poverty I was enclosed in. This knowledge led me through a lot of hurdles I had to scale to get to the point I wanted to be at in life.

I knew from an early age that school was not really my thing. I was not daft, and when I really concentrated, I was a smart student. As a matter of fact, once in fifth grade, I won an award for a science project where I had done an assignment on the human tongue. It was so good that the teachers had no choice but to give me an award; as a result, I was considered to have passed the subject already. My challenge with school and academics was mostly hinged on the fact that I had ADHD, and it was diagnosed when I was still relatively young. As opposed to what many people thought about me and my academics, sports was one of my favorite things. I never hesitated to join in any sporting activity I could; and many times, I was a part of street football, basketball, and the likes. Although I was forming into an impressive young man, I still knew I could not live the life that was looming ahead of me. I wanted more, and just a college certificate was not going to get me what I wanted.

With this knowledge, I knew I had to take inventory of my skills and begin to work on something that was more extra-curricular and which had more bearings as regards where I saw myself going to in the years to come. I think my major awakening in finance came from the pictures I had seen over time. There remains this episode of the picture of stocks I saw in the local newspaper a long time ago.

This point of inventory taking was when I really began to discover that I was quite good at graphics designing and visuals. This was because I was meticulous, and not a lot of things were left unnoticed whenever I went to work on a particular project. Next to my graphics skills, I was also a good artist in the sense that I could draw well. The result of this was that I was spotted by the local TV and in no time, I was among those few people that were picked to go and start interning with the local TV station. Following this, I got opportunities to work on many newspapers, stations, and allied organizations.

When I was about 10 or 11, I was spotted out and made the captain of the football team in my area. The organizer said it was because I was very good at it; and also owing to the fact that I had nature and good looks on my side. I was forming up to be one muscular young man; and even at that age, it was evident that I was not just one scrawny kid. Banking on that stroke of grace, my mom decided I was good for something more than street football; and she signed me up for pup football. Pup football was the league for younger and relatively inexperienced people who were not old enough to play in any real league. Although it was a pup league, it was a useful ground for training and exposing me to many more things that played a pivotal role in my life.

The first time I appeared for the pup meeting, I could not seem to stay after my mom left to return home. For some reason, I felt a bit lost. Tearing myself away from the boys playing sports all around me, I ran as quickly as my legs could carry me back to my mother, who was surprised to see that I had refused to stay for the meeting. Inasmuch as I did not want to be part of the meeting with the guys, my mother made me stay for that pup session, and she made sure that I attended all that followed as much as possible. This was an unwelcome development for me at first, but I was unable to know at the time that what she was doing was mainly for my good. As things turned out, I learned a few lessons that guide me for the rest of my life from my association with those guys at the pup sessions.

As I kept on moving, there was a need for me to get a job. I was about 16 when this need arose. This was a result of the fact that I have always been an independent person who would rather try to solve his problems himself than roll over responsibility to others. When I was ready to get this job, I went off in search of a job. Unfortunately, I was unable to have much luck with this job-seeking expedition, as all the places I applied to did not get back to me. Shortly before I ran out of patience, I was visited by a little stroke of luck. One of the places I applied to, replied to me; and they were ready to hire me, but there was a challenge. The opening that was available was only for someone who was at least 18. I was going to pull back from taking the job since I was only 16 at the time, but there was just something about it that pulled me in.

Instead of declining the job offer, I pulled off a little prank and altered the date on my birth certificate. Because I already had nature and genetics on my side, it was not hard for me to pull it off. So, with a certificate that showed that I was two years above what I truly was, I went in search of that job. The interview went well, and I was hired for the job.

My attention to detail and good work ethic singled me out before my bosses. In no time, they were ready to promote me, and though I was as happy as I could get, I knew there was no need to sweat it. As a result of the fear that accompanied the knowledge of what I had done, I quit the job because I did not want them to find out that I had added a few years to my original age. Much to the chagrin of my bosses, I slipped away from their grasp and returned to the life I had all along. While all this happened, I never lost my flair for football, and all through high school I played on the team with boys my age. Mingling with boys my age; that was the beginning of my problems.

As we approached the end of high school, I began to interact with a group of boys that were bad news. Although I knew I was making a grave mistake, I was riding on the high of acceptance and the grudging respect I got from the crowd of boys I hung out with. Because they were always making me feel as though I was important, while still placing a subtle pressure on me to meet up with them and what they were known for. My transition years were the most tumultuous for me because during this timeframe I began to indulge in a lot of things that were both wrong and completely unsuitable for where I saw myself going to in life.

Smoking

Drinking

Cutting classes

You name it, and I was probably involved in it at this time in my life. In my defense, I had a lot going on in my life at the same time – with my health challenge, trying to juggle and balance every other part of my life was a war. At this point of my life, I also had to battle with that nagging feeling in me that told me that I was a huge disappointment. Knowing that my family was not wealthy, and having to make a mess of all the efforts of everyone who cared as much as to make an input in my life cut deeper than anything, but I was set on a path for a very long time. It may be a result of youthful exuberance, but after a series of night school and summer programs, I was able to complete high school and get my diploma. This was a major miracle because at the time, there were not a lot of black men I knew who had a diploma, at least not in my area. Still trying to find out exactly who I was and how I was going to shed all the things that were bothering me, I decided I was going to get into college and at least continue my education.

There may have been a lot going on with me, but one thing I was certain of was the fact that I was not going to end up where the people around me ended up or seemed to end up. There seemed to be this satisfaction with poverty amongst my people. As I discovered, not a lot of people made efforts to become better than what was obtainable and become financially free. I knew that was not my thing, and I had to do drastic stuff if I was going to be able to achieve my dreams.

The Defining Moment

The defining moment in my life's journey came when I least expected it. I was barely in college and battling with the fair share of demons I was allocated by life when it happened. Because of the many things that surrounded me and the habits I was indulging myself in, I had to drop out of school. My health condition was in no way helping me, and when ADHD meets with a person who is already distracted and has his attention on other things, the results are usually bad. This was what I was able to discover with my life.

Still reeling from the blow that came with having to drop out of school and feeling sorry for myself, I was greeted with the worst news that played a major role in breaking me. My father died! He was killed in an accident, more like a hit-and-run accident, and there was basically no hope for the person who was responsible for the accident to be found and justice to be served. This was a challenging time for all of us at home; my mother and my siblings, too, were struck by this blow as much as I was struck by it. Because of the sudden exit of my father, I was forced to take up some roles I was not yet prepared for. Being the man of the family was hard work, and because of this, I had to join the workforce again while my mates were back in school learning what I had misused the chance to learn.

This new emphasis on work and the urgent need for cash made me revisit old lifestyles I had planned to ditch as I grew up. These lifestyles I revisited included smoking weed and selling drugs. During this phase of my life, I focused on selling coke, weed, and everything in between. The result was that I was making quite a good sum of money from both ventures – my regular job and the illicit moving of drugs around the 'hood. At this young age, money began to flow to me well, because there is actual money in this act of selling drugs illicitly.

I had a group of friends I moved with at this time of my life. We were quite tight, and as I would love to think, we ran the 'hood together. At this point, I was so loyal to them, and we would spend time thinking and planning how we were going to make the next move of our contraband goods away from the 'hood and into the hands of the people that needed them. As a result of my physical looks, and the fact that I always had a spark of leadership qualities, I unofficially became the leader of this group.

Over time, as we got deeper into what we were doing, I miraculously kept my job; and this other thing we were doing was moving well, for me, at least. My friends didn't have it badly, but it was obvious I was getting much more than they were. For some reason, this kept happening, but I did all I could during this time to make sure that they knew that I was still rooting for them. This made me go out of my way to try to prove my loyalty to them on several occasions, to the extent that I did not mind giving any of them the shirt off my back as proof. As we proceeded, I had this nagging feeling that they were beginning to get jealous of me and the money I was getting from my two endeavors. It did not help that I was easy on the eyes and had a lot of lady folk flocking in my direction.

I was literally the definition of a successful, young black man. I had money, I had the looks, and I had a decent source of income, for those who did not know what they could not see. Because of the steady influx of females around me, I got well-acquainted with one of these ladies; and in my 20s, I had a son.

A Worse Downward Spiral

At this point, it looked as though life was at its best. Although I had not completed college, it looked as though I had a shot at doing something worthwhile with my life. The only thing was that I was not prepared for the curveball life was about to toss in my direction.

This was shortly after I had my son. There was a party away from the 'hood, which I attended that night. I was supposed to have gone with the boys; but at the last moment, most of them declined the party with one or more excuses. At the end of the day, I had only one person to go with. Throughout the party, I could not get rid of the feeling that I was missing out on something serious, and that my life was about to change forever. I shoved this feeling away whenever it came up and went on with the party. During this time, I did notice that the person who I came with to the party was behaving funny and was texting on the phone throughout the night. After a night of partying, I got back to my house just to meet a state of disarray.

Everything that could be stolen had been stolen. Every last bit of money I had was taken, every valuable carted away with, and all that was left in the house were things that were not useful to me.

As I stood in the midst of the rubble that early morning, I felt my heart shatter into a million tiny shards; and it was as though there was nowhere to run away from the stress that was closing in on me. Deciding that there was no need to cry over spilled milk, I went to work and pulled a few stunts with the contacts I had. What I learned after the investigation was strong enough to make me cynical for the rest of my life. The theft was masterminded and executed by those friends of mine who had bailed on me on the night of the party. As a matter of fact, the plan was for the one who went with me to be a sentry and ensure that I was occupied throughout the night while communicating with the rest of the cartel. As much as I felt hurt by everything I learned, I decided I was not going to take any physical action on them.

The investigation also revealed that these same people had been sneaking around behind my back and getting frisky with the same girls I was either involved with or planning to get involved with. Although this was not a problem for me, because I could not have all the ladies in the 'hood; it further revealed the darkness in the hearts of the people I considered my friends. After learning this, I knew I had to change my friends' circle and at least try to be a good dad for my son.

This downward spiral was going to be the springboard to take me upwards once again.

Making U-Turns and My Journey to Sanity Once Again

This incident with the 'friends' had forced me to take stock of my life. Inasmuch as I felt bad about what they had done to me; I learned a lot of invaluable lessons, and I decided that it was time to make a change for good. As I realized, not a lot of drug dealers have great endings, and it was only sane for me to begin to think of how to become better before I landed myself in something much worse. I figured that all the things they had taken away from me were the things I had gotten through less than questionable means, and they were not mine at the end of the day. With this new knowledge, I resolved to get myself involved in new stuff and be a legitimately wealthy person. This decision is what heralded my comeback and spurred me into looking for ways to become better for all the people around me.

My new desire to be a better person led me into searching for business opportunities and career paths that could make me the same returns as one who was almost becoming big in the drug peddling industry. As a guy who had tasted the good life, and had the opportunity to spend money; I never wanted to return to the life of penury – at least I did not want to return there without a solid escape plan. This research yielded answers, and I found that the career paths that could get me the financial independence I yearned for were pro sporting, becoming the CEO of a major corporation, or becoming a stockbroker.

These thoughts were only facilitated by Hurricane Katrina as I assessed the level of damage that was done; and thought to myself, the amount of money that wood-making companies were about to make out of the whole situation was massive. It became a part of my thoughts that whoever owned a part of the wood-making industry by owning shares or stocks in a company was going to make a large profit out of the whole situation. As a result of these thoughts, I was completely invested in the idea of becoming a stockbroker; and the bulk of what I knew came from dedicating my time to watching stock channels and reading everything I could find that was related.

My research and fascination with this discipline led me to television shows upon shows. It was on one of these episodes that I stumbled across Jim Cramer, who was an investment guru. He simplified the whole process of investing and took the edge off it. As I kept following his works, I discovered that investing was not as herculean a task as many people made it seem. This was because Jim made it seem as simple as it could get. As I kept interacting with him and his content, my interest in the field began to increase; and I began to purchase more books and go out of my way to ensure that I was making the most out of my new venture. One of the first books I purchased in this field was "Investing in the Market for Dummies."

This book opened me up to many things that I did not know. As I kept on moving, I decided it was time I make a drastic move because I had learned that without taking action, I was not going to achieve anything worthwhile. This led me into investing my money in the market. I waited this long because although I knew investing was the right and most profitable thing I could do, almost all the content I interacted with peddled the idea that you needed a broker to invest. My experiences prior to this time had taught me that although there may have been some truth in this, there was no need for me to depend on a middleman. I had been cheated of my money before; and I was not eager to repeat the experience, because I had learned that there were quite a number of hoodlums hiding behind the thick fabrics of suits.

This decision made me sink my teeth deeper into the market. I discovered ways through which I could invest without the use of a middleman, and most of these seemed to have reduced risk levels, so I was game. After a prolonged season of learning and studying, I purchased my stocks through some platforms. The returns I got from that transaction seemed good and were encouraging to me. I nursed dreams of opening my own business and entering the market as a big name. After performing this transaction and a series of others that were quite successful, I decided that I wanted to spend my life doing this – not just making money, but making people around the world like me see that there are other options. I decided that it was time to teach chil dren from lower-class families, who grew up in ghettos and wrong neighborhoods, that there are other ways to make money besides drugs, whoring themselves out, and the vices that are mainstream in these areas.

It is for this single reason that I wrote this book. In this book, I teach you proven strategies for investment. What many people fail to understand is that despite how it is presented, investing is based on one principle—the principle of buying for a low price and selling at a higher price. Over time, this principle has been applied to almost everything–sales of everyday household products, stocks, and everything in between.

Looking back, I realize that although I put in a lot of work to get to where I am today; when contrasted against the life I used to live, that one pales in comparison. This is the life that is much better because I can go to sleep at night without having a voice nagging at the back of my mind reminding me of the hideous things I had done throughout the day. I have learned a lot within the time frame, and that is what I seek to teach anyone that will learn. There is no need to take the wrong path searching for finances and financial resources. This much, I learned by myself.

So, this book is dedicated to you.

If you have ever wondered how you can get out of the life of poverty and achieve your financial dreams, then the following pages are for you. You can choose to drop this book now and try out different things, but remember that your life is passing by and time won't wait. In this book, I will save you years of trying and failing. So, if you need to find proven ways to invest without involving the services of a middleman (who may or may not swindle you of your hard-earned resources); then you need to keep reading, as you will find this book an invaluable tool on your journey to financial freedom.

2

BASIC INVESTING

You have heard many financial experts and money coaches shed light on the value of investing as you journey to financial freedom. You have heard about investing from all directions, you can possibly hear it from – jingles on radio, announcements and training sessions being aired on TV, from the mini flashes of pop-up ads you encounter every day as you journey through the internet, in books, and the list is endless. The thing is conditioning has taught many people not to take these seriously enough or how to do it.

This is because when these announcements and reminders on how vital it is to invest are made, they are usually followed up by sales pitches of coaches who want you to come under their wings and tutelage. In many cases, when a sales pitch is not made, the value of the information being passed may not be as valuable and comprehensive as it should be.

These methods of delivery leave many things to be desired, but the messages behind them are actually true.

Although it is good to have coaches and mentors in any sphere, it is up to you to decide whether you are going to be successful in the venture. You can still learn how to invest, become good at the art of investing, carry out your first investment exercise and the many after that and record returns on investments - all by yourself.

As I mentioned in the chapter that led up to this, I learned the art of investing and decided to invest on my own the first time I wanted to invest. The better part was that this investment exercise was successful, and I found the processes and systems to be repeatable.

In this chapter, you will be exposed to the rudiments of investing. You will learn the basics and the foundations of the trade, and you will learn what you need to do for your investments to make sense and yield quantum returns. If you're in the market for some qualitative, practical knowl edge on how you can start investing (which you are, or you wouldn't have read this far), you will continue reading through the pages, because there is a lot of quality content. If, on the other hand, you are not seeking this kind of information; well, the book is already in your hands, so it's best you continue reading so as to gain this knowledge. Who knows when you will finally need it?

First Words

My first words creating financial freedom were the skills that helped me get to where I am today. They were a major part of the skills I deployed. Learning my first words, and getting very good at them, made me become a practical man, a deep thinker, and a man who paid attention to strategies, processes, and top-quality information.

Early in my life, work projects bothered me so much that I could hardly get my head into the game anytime I tried to work eight hours a day. I used to feel so worked up that I spent a sizeable quota of those days doing something which was entirely different from whatever it was I was supposed to do.

My life began to take an upward turn when I learned this first financial freedom word and mastered the skill of investing. This skill came from several long hours, days, weeks, and months of intense learning, searching over the internet, and consulting with various books on the subject of investing. I learned how to make my money multiply and last longer when my father passed. This was because there arose a lot of challenges; and as a result,, spending became inevitable and sometimes erratic on my part.

At this point, my family had real estate of various forms. But in my way of not seeing that I had been blessed with a goldmine, I spent all that I could find on living a flashy lifestyle; spending unnecessarily on clothes, cars, and the rest of them. After a few years of making bad choices and crazy investment decisions, I was neck-deep in being broke. I had lost almost everything I could find and almost everything I had received from my father. I think that losing all the homes we had and losing almost all the valuable property I had inherited and been given by various family members fueled my passion to learn the best and safest ways to invest, and not stand the chance of losing the things that mattered the most to me. I look back on this period of my life with gratitude because it was the final push I needed to get started on putting my life back together.

From these experiences, I learned five invaluable les

sons. I hope these will be useful to you on your journey toward building financial stability.

1. **It does not so much matter when and how you fall, what matters is whether you decide to get up or not.**

   This may sound like a cliché, but I can tell you that it is one of the best pieces of advice you will ever get. If you have been reading this book with rapt attention up until this point, then you must know that I have made my fair share of mistakes in life; mistakes I will not bother going through again.

   It does not matter whether or not you make mistakes; what matters is that you are able to learn from those mistakes and make better decisions in light of the new person you are. So, the next time you make financial mistakes, try not to sit on your behind and waste a lot of quality time crying and mourning your fate. Rather, get up and make the most out of it, learn the lessons, and be on your way to a better place in your finances and investment skills.

2. **To be successful, you must learn how to be passionate, driven, and ambitious.**

Many people cringe at the mention of the word "ambitious," but they do not know that this is what separates many people from the actualization of their big dream. You will only be spurred towards becoming a much better person and reach your financial goals if you master the art of being ambitious and driven. Ambition feeds your passion as you journey to the place of financial freedom. Remember one thing I told you; I spent valuable time researching and learning what I am about to share with you. This was only possible because I had a drive, and it was something I looked forward to.

What I looked forward to most was to be financially independent for the rest of my life, give my children something to hold on to which would serve as a head start in life, and to pass on this knowledge to as many as would receive it from me. This was an ambition, and it has kept me going all these years.

3. **You need a keen eye for details.**

If you are going to be successful and achieve financial independence in your life, you must be able to observe – not just look, but actually see. Seeing, in this context, applies to your ability to notice things that are not being said and begin to apply them. You must know that not everything you need to be a successful person in terms of your finances will be taught in books and shown in classes. You must develop a keen eye that looks far deeper within yourself and is able to make decisions. Also, stop listening to what you are being told by teachers and some tutors and begin to observe them. The idea is to find out HOW they live and not just listen to what they say. When you are armed with this knowledge, you can begin to take steps in the right direction.

4. **Learn to ask questions – smart questions.**

"Curiosity killed the cat" is a common saying that does more harm than good in our world. You will not get to the top and be on top of your financial game if you do not master the art of asking smart, challenging, and reasonable questions. This skill is what helps you make sense of the things that you come in contact with and find out how they relate to you and your life. As you journey to financial freedom, do not just be the one who swallows everything he is fed – hook, line, and sinker. Be the one who asks the right questions and collects valuable information. This is one of the best skills you will learn as you begin your journey to financial independence.

5. **Change your mindset about financial independence and about money in general.**

Taking an assessment of my neighborhood and the people who grew up and lived where I did, I discovered that one of their major challenges was a limiting mind-set about money. It seemed there was some rule that people never spoke about money. Every person I knew seemed satisfied with their level of wealth, and as a result of that, it was impossible to grow past that level. If you are not yet able to adjust your mindset on an issue and sustain this change, you will not be able to see the changes in your life.

Some people do not become financially independent because a part of them just does not believe that there is something in it for them. They cannot come to terms with the fact that they are deserving and the result is that they never get what they want – which in this case is financial independence. Let this be your first task; get your mindset right, and then you can go on into the other things you must do to kiss poverty goodbye.

The Basics of Investing

Basic investing is a fancy name given to the concept of investing. This implies that investing and basic investing means the same thing. The thing is that there may be a difference in the size of the investments and the commitments they require on both sides. As an introduction, basic investing is the art and act of buying investments. This implies that investing is the act of buying over anything that can yield profitable returns to you as the days unfold. When put in simpler terms, investing is the practice of committing your money and other valuable resources with the intentions of gaining valuable returns. In the world of investment, you put in something smaller with respect to what you have your eyes on, with intentions of gaining something bigger and more valuable with time and the passage of other valuable, yet variable, resources. The goal of investment in all respects is to help you reach a goal you have set faster and to help you make more money.

Here is the thing you should know about investment. It may come in various forms and take on many different expressions; but when looked at objectively, investing is built off the same principle. This means that notwithstanding where you put your money – with a government organization, a corporate body, an independently run business, and all other places you can invest in, the goal is the same. This aim is to get your money to increase so that after a while, you have more than you put into your investment.

As a rule of thumb, what you get for investing is ALWAYS bigger in terms of quality, quantity, and value than what you put in in the first place. That is why it is known as investing.

A common form of investing a few years back was the practice of buying stamps; that is, collecting vintage stamps and keeping them over time as they gained value. As their price increased, whoever had them could then bring them out and resell at a price much higher than what they were bought for in the first place. Aside from this, collecting certain sports equipment can be considered investing. For example, baseball and basketball cards are considered investing if collected, kept, and returned to the marketplace at the proper time. Art is also a great place to invest. This is because some paintings are worth millions of dollars today, and these paintings are possessed by the elite few. Just imagine for one moment that you attended a yard sale or random auction event and a painting caught your attention. Imagine that you put your hands into your pockets and paid for this painting without knowing that what you bought is worth millions. Imagine that a random person walks into your house a few days later and tells you the exact value of that painting that is now hanging above the mantelpiece in your living room. Imagine for one minute what you do with that painting when you discover this.

Inasmuch as the scenarios painted above may seem a bit too good to be true, many people have stumbled into great opportunities that changed their financial statuses just like these. The goal of this section is not just to make you aware that there are these opportunities lying around you, but to spur you into action so that you begin to research and see the limitless opportunities that lie around you when you know exactly what it means to invest and how to do that the right way. Consider these and more to be slices in your investment pizza that increase in value and price over time. The earlier you learn how to amass these little pieces that seem inconsequential and keep them until the right time to return them to the marketplace for much more value than you bought them for, the better it is for you. This art is the simple process through which a powerful investor portfolio is built.

Why you should understand investing and how it is done the right way.

It is not enough to know that the concept and practice of investing will help you achieve your financial goals and get to the place of financial freedom faster, you must know how to invest and how to do it the right way. Many people give up on the idea of investing and even write it off as being scam because they do not understand the risks involved in this venture. Neither have they decided to take time and study what it is they are doing.

There are several reasons why you must take the time to understand the world of investment and learn how to do it the right way. In this section, we cover a few of these reasons.

1. **Your money is involved.**

   There is no sugar coating this one. As we pointed out earlier, one of the major reasons people do not make the most out of the investment world is that they fail to understand what it is all about. Take this as inspiration the next time you are about to invest in anything – your money is involved.

   Unless you are giving to charity, or you have a great deal of money that you can afford to flush some very well-needed notes down the drain, then you must study this world and how it works. Let's be real with ourselves. You came to invest because you are looking for avenues to grow your finances and achieve a state of financial independence quickly. It will only be counter-productive if you end up investing in something and it ends up failing – all because you did not study the market.

Remember, the goal of investing is to help your money grow; and just like in real life, there are specific things you must know to make the most out of your investment. This is why you need to understand this concept well and know how this industry works.

2. **Investing is a highly sought after skill** and provides you with a competitive edge. Over the years, and as history unfolds, we have seen many industries swallowed up by other industries that predicted their future and invested so heavily in them that they became the principal shareholders. This shows the value that comes with being an investor with keen eyes.

Investing is one skill that can differentiate a good business person from an exceptional businessman. While a good businessman may know little to nothing on the subject, the exceptional businessman with a great business empire understands the value of knowing how to invest. With this skill in his bag of infinite tricks, he is equipped to enlarge the frontiers of his industry, capture and conquer new grounds as a businessman, and generally live the life of his dreams.

The skill of investing is also necessary because it can be applied to other areas of your life to yield many more results. For instance, an investment in a budding friendship/relationship can turn into an investment that is worth millions of dollars in the future.

Many multi-billion business conglomerates know this; and that is why they are always on the prowl, looking for new grounds to cover and new and viable places to invest. As far as relationships go, many of the corporations you admire today were started by visionary people who were friends but had an idea to change the world. With the right strategies applied consistently over time, they reached the point where they are. This is how investing in good relationships can be instrumental to changing a person's life.

3. **Investing gets you closer to financial freedom** faster than most white-collar jobs. There is no voodoo to this. If your goal is to reach financial freedom – in that you can do anything you want, at any time you want to, without having to deal with the financial constraints – then one of the best ways to meet this goal is by investing in a viable place. Inasmuch as we often fail to admit this, one of the major ways to end up with no plans for our financial future is to put all our confidence on a pay sheet that will be signed by a boss. This not only places a clamp on how much money a person can make as he works his life away; it keeps financial independence far away.

Investing is one way to get to your financial independence goal faster. Since the market is heavily dependent on how well what you invest in will yield for you, there is no limit as to the amount of money that can be cashed out from one of these investment returns if all goes well.

4. **Investing is one of the surest ways of creating passive income** and having your money grow. The concept of passive income is one that cannot be overemphasized. The thoughts of having your mon-

ey grow while you still have the time to get involved with other things that really matter to you are too good for many people to pass up. As a result, investing is one of the best ways to generate passive income.

First things first; what is passive in come?

Passive income is the name given to money you make without working or engaging in a money-making activity. As opposed to active income, which requires that you be up and about the task at hand, such as selling your products/services as a business person, sales prospecting, and all the rest of them; passive income is made while you are not engaging in these money-making activities.

Liken your investment to the seeds that are planted during the rainy season. Although the farmer who plants them will not stay on the farm and watch them grow; he can still return to the farm when the time is right, knowing that there is a great harvest there. This is because, during the time he was not at the farm, his seeds kept on growing. This is the same thing that happens whenever you invest in the right place.

Your money grows with time, and although you may not be there, you know that when the investment period is up, you will be making much more than you put in. This is the best part of investing – still making money even when you are not actively at work.

The skill of investing, if learned well and applied, is a win-win. It applies farther than money and the investment world. This skill is useful in all ramifications. The goal of this book is to break it down and show you how you can get the best results.

Starting With Investing

Here are the first steps you must take if you want to start with investing the right way.

1. Begin from the Beginning

Everything we know had a start; even the world we live in had a beginning. Investing blindly is not good and will not give you any results if you do not understand the concept and start on the right track.

Now that you have made up your mind to invest, it is time to start off at the right place. Where exactly is the beginning in this context, and how do I start there, you may ask? This is all you need to know.

Beginning in this context refers to all the work you need to do to have a great investor experience. This step entails that you take some time off to have serious conversations with yourself to ensure you are doing the right thing. Here are a few steps you need to take:

2. **Define Your Goals**

   What exactly are you looking to achieve in this industry and path? If you do not have goals articulated and clearly written down, you have no way to discover if you are making progress or not. This is the challenge that many people have. They get into investing with no goals; and as a result, they are frustrated in their journeys. While you define what your goals are, be sure to answer these questions as clearly and honestly as you can.

   - **What am I doing here?** Why have I chosen to walk this, of all paths? The answer to this question makes sure you stay on course and do not give up along the way.

- **As I begin my journey into the world of investing,** what does a success look like to me? The answers you give yourself determine what you celebrate as success. Your answers should be along the lines of more money, having more time to do the things I love, financial freedom and independence, etc.

- **Now that you have clearly defined goals,** the next step is to ensure that you are willing to put in the work. As we have discussed earlier, investing is not something you do without thinking it through. At this stage of your journey, you must be willing and ready to ask and answer these questions.

- **What exactly do I know about investing?** Since this is a venture you want to go into, you must be completely honest with yourself. The answer to this question informs the next set of decisions and actions you take.

- **What can I do to become a better investor?** The reason you are venturing into this world of investing is that you have financial dreams, and you need to be a great investor if you meet those needs. To be a better investor, there are specific actions you must be willing to do and dogged about taking. These may include getting tutored by successful investors, getting yourself into a network of people who have the same passion as you do, getting yourself to become a better investor by learning, etc. This step helps you get action steps so you know exactly how to start.

- **What do I know about this market?** This is where you put pen to paper and begin to ask the difficult questions. If you do not ask and answer these questions before you begin, you will end up making a mess of yourself. This is where you identify those things that stand as a hindrance to the success of your investor journey and plug all the holes.

- **What am I willing to put** in order to become the best investor there is, or to at least never lose out on my investments? What is the exact amount of research I am willing to put in? How am I going to go about it? Am I even willing to do the work, or not? When you have answered these questions, you will know what the best line of action is for you.

2. **Understand the Principles Involved in This Venture**

Studies show that many people make mistakes that

leave them too scared to try again, simply because they do not understand the venture they are pursuing. If you are going to be a successful investor, you must spend time understanding the principles that guide your field of discipline before you get started with investing.

Imagine for one second that someone walks off the edge of a bridge not knowing that there is a law in the earth called gravity. Do you think that the planet will have mercy on him because he did not know that he was going to fall? Absolutely not. He will fall off that bridge and into the water. Many times he will plummet to his death – all because he failed to understand that there are laws that guide the place he is in.

In the same way, there are laws that guide this venture of investing. If you are going to make massive progress, you must understand these laws and see exactly how they apply to the market. With a deep, working knowledge of them, you will know how what you have to do and where you should get involved. One of these is the law of compound interest.

What is compound interest, and how does it apply to investing?

In the banking and investment industries, compound interest is defined as interest, such as on a loan or bank account, which is calculated on the total of the principal plus the interest accumulated over time. This implies that compound interest is a combination of multiple interests that gather over time on the same investment.

Compound interest, more accurately known as compounding, is a viable system through which the money you are trying to invest can grow. This happens when you put money into any scheme; and when the initial returns come, you re-invest the returns so that you can get something much bigger than you started out with. If done properly, compounding is one method many investment giants have used to build their fortunes; and you can adopt this method, too. One of the best ways to begin investing is to start out with stocks.

Another principle you must learn if you will be a good investor is the principle of taking risks. Here is the truth of the matter:

The investment market is one of the most volatile markets in the world. It takes a lot of guts to put your money and the things you value into something you are not sure will give you the returns you seek. This is why you need to understand that investing is a risk, and you are willing to address it as such. No matter how careful you are, there is always that tendency that your investments may not pay off; but as the saying goes, if you do not have the guts, then there will be no glory.

To be a successful investor and reach your aim to build the life of your dreams, you must be able and willing to take risks.

- **Get all you need before you start.** There is a common saying that if you fail to plan, then you have automatically planned to fail. This saying holds true, especially in investing. Before you start, you must know exactly the things you need and do a thorough job of gathering them all.

- As a rule of thumb, try to be as debt-free as you can before you invest. Unless you are already financially stable, investing may take away your monetary resources in the meantime. For this reason, you may want to begin by making sure you are debt-free.

Also, gather all the knowledge you need to thrive in this industry. If you venture into this place without guidance, you will be stripped of all you have and left out in the cold to die. Your equipping, and how well you prepare yourself, goes a long way to ensure that you are successful as an investor. When you are done, you need to decide how much time you want to spend on your investments. Some investments need you to constantly look at them to be sure that things are going well, while others do not need that much attention. Find out the ones that suit your needs and go for them.

Auto-pilot investing is one of those types of investments that do not necessarily need you to be always on the lookout for them. All you need to do there is check-up occasionally to ensure that things are still on track. These are generally considered to be safer investments. Examples of this kind are bonds. Bonds are certificates that are issued by the government and governing bodies of organizations, showing that the bearer of the certificate is entitled to receive an amount of money over time. Bonds are great because they are not necessarily affected by inflation and other market determinants.

While reading this book, you will come across several terms. These terms are common in the market (that is the investment industry); and as a result of that, it will be wise if we begin by defining them.

Common concepts in the investment world:

1. Compound Interest (compounding)

Although we threw a little light on this earlier, let us take a more in-depth look. Compounding is a foundational concept in the world of investing. This is because of how far and how fast money can grow over an expanded period. As discussed earlier, compounding is the process through which money that has been put in an investment scheme is left there; and even after the first return is due, it is returned back into that scheme to yield more. The result of this is that the returns that come over time increase on all fronts; and depending on the quality of what is invested in, the money will only keep on increasing.

Compounding is simply the way your money makes more money for you. Take this instance. If you make an investment worth $1000, and you are to get a reward of about $200 after a 20-day period of time; this implies that after 20 days, you will have $1200 (all things being equal). Compounding works like this.

Since you were entitled to a 20 percent increase at first, if you decide to reinvest that $1200, after another 20 days, you will still get 20 percent back, and this time 20 percent is $240. If this continues, you will amass an amount of money that is a far cry away from what you started with. This is how it works in a nutshell.

Remember that we discussed you should not think of investing if you are in debt? You may have been confused as to what that means. Well, this is one reason why it is unadvisable to do such a thing. Compound interest is wonderful when it is working on your side; but when it is on the other end of the equation (working against you), it is detrimental and can keep you from reaching your financial goals. This is how it works.

If you borrow money, say on your credit card or from any financial house, you are charged interest on your interest. This implies that the amount you have to pay as interest is compounded per day, as the systems check how much debt you have on that card and revise the interest you must pay as a result of compounding. So, the longer this debt stretches out, the worse it gets for you; because at the end of a prolonged season, you may be shocked to discover that the interest you now have to pay may be bigger than the money you borrowed. This is the main reason why you need to make sure that compounding is working in your favor and not against you.

This is the reason many people have gone broke and been pulled into unnecessary debt. They did not know that compound interest can work against them, and the result of this is that they end up making mistakes that are worse than what they have made if they had not borrowed in the first place. In a nutshell, it is advisable to always be debt-free, especially as you venture into becoming an investor.

2. **Bonds**

You hear the term again and again. Bonds! What are bonds and how do they relate to investing?

You may have heard of the concept of loans before now. A loan is an amount of money that is lent to someone over time. The reason for this is to invest in something, while the person doing the loaning receives back his principle, alongside some interest that has been accrued. This is the same concept that bonds are built upon.

A bond is a document (fixed income instrument) which represents the details of a transaction and is used as a token to signify that the bearer is entitled to receive some amount of remuneration at the end of a predetermined time interval. This implies that when a bond is issued to someone, it shows that the person, just like an investor or lender, has put an amount of his money into an organization (government-owned or private sector). As a result of this, he is entitled to receive a fraction of the financial benefits that come from investing his money in that firm for a period of time which is specified in the bond.

Bonds are used by any and every governmental body you can think of – states, municipalities, corporate organizations, etc. – to fund projects and keep the daily operation of the organization together. Once they are able to get people to buy bonds in their project, these people become investors or debt-holders; and the contract details exactly how much of the money that comes out of the project or organization they are entitled to earn over a period of time.

Bonds are assets, and their prices are inversely proportional. When bond rates hike, the prices of bonds go down, and the reverse is the case on the other hand. Since bonds pay a fixed-interest rate to those who have them, they are seen as fixed-income instruments. This implies that notwithstanding how bad or how great the economy is, having bonds with a company is a great way to get a fixed amount of money coming your way on a regular basis.

3. **Mutual Funds**

A mutual fund is a financial vehicle that gives the possessor access to professionally managed portfolios of investments that have the yielding power in them. A mutual fund is usually made up of a variety of investments, which all have specific parts to play. In a typical mutual fund, there are many assets including stocks, bonds, money market instruments, equities, and more. The aim of mutual funds, just like every other thing we have discussed, is to raise money for the investor.

The investor in this context is the person who has the portfolio, or who the portfolio is being run for. Because of the diversity in this form of investment terrain, it is usually advisable that a person who is not into the investment sector get a professional to manage this investment for him. Mutual funds are investments collected from different investors that drive various projects and keep things going smoothly within a context. When these are collected, they are channeled into a common area which is considered a mutual working space. The mutual working space consists of many types of investments.

Remember that we said that investments are driven towards the actualization of a target, and as a result, mutual funds are communally run. The success of every mutual fund is dependent on the way every person who has a part in the mutual fund makes use of his own. Mutual funds are an aggregation of many investments, and the easiest way to check whether there is success in the fund is by checking the total market cap of the fund. The total market cap is derived by looking at the aggregate of the performance of the individual and underlying investments that are a part of the mutual fund.

4. Index Funds

These have something in common with mutual funds — they are obtained as a result of the aggregation of many smaller units.

An index fund is a type of mutual fund — this is the first thing you should know about index funds. Index funds can also be looked at as a form of exchange-traded funds (ETFs), in which there is a portfolio that is made to track the components of a financial market index.

Index funds work by mimicking the activities of the stock and finance market. As a matter of fact, the legendary investor — Warren Buffet — has discussed that mutual funds are a great tool to make sure a person gets out of financial struggles, especially in the latter parts of his life. This is because, instead of having to buy investments one at a time and counting the costs involved — in terms of market timing, risks, possible failures, and losses/wins — a person can study the market and make a more safe investment in index funds which, as we have discussed, are made up of sub-units or individual investments.

The secret to indexing is in the ability to have keen eyes and be able to spot what ticks in the marketplace. Considering the work involved in getting this type of investment to work, and all the risks in it, it is usually advisable that the job be outsourced to fund portfolio managers – who are people with working knowledge and experience in the investment market and have what it takes to make expert decisions and have in-depth insights into the marketplace. They are specialists, and they are usually the best bet when it comes to making sure that there is little to no damage taken by the investors.

Fund managers handle indexing funds by taking a good look at the marketplace. They see what is obtainable; and with that knowledge, they build a portfolio with individual investment holdings mirroring the securities of a particular index. The goal of this is to alter the trajectory of the stock market as a whole, or a very reasonable section of it, with hopes that this change will favor their index funds by matching it in performance as well.

There is one thing quite common about mutual and index funds. This is the fact that they invest in multi ple stocks at once, and as a result, they are a bit riskier to be invested in. This concept is called weighted investing, and in this scenario, money is spread out over different stocks. The benefit is there is a vast array of investment options to go by, the propensity for making gains is increased, and as a result, the investor stands a better chance of gaining much more than he ever invested in the first place. But as said earlier, the risks here are considerably more, and as a result of this, it is advisable to get a financial expert to make these decisions and help you get started – especially if you are new to the investment world.

Understanding these will make your journey through the world of investing a whole lot easier.

5. **Stock/Bond Investing**

Stock investing is the practice of investing in stocks. This is achieved by purchasing stocks in a company and is a major way to ensure that you never get out of financial supplies again in your life. When you buy stocks/bonds in a company, you are ushered into the company of those who own stocks/bonds in the company – and these are the people who own different percentages of the company. As a result of this, you are a part of the owners of the company. The more stock/bonds you own in a company, the more of the company you own and the more you are an indispensable part of the company board.

Stock investing is one way to ensure that you hit your financial goals and become free in your money and wealth. This is because stock investing is considered relatively less-risky, and if you are investing in a feasible company that is well-known and does their homework, you end up gaining so much more than you put in. Many people become much bigger stock investors by investing in companies they perceive will go up in value. If this happens and the company does go up in value, they end up making much more than they would have. But to be successful in this venture, there are things you must be aware of, including the fact that there is no eliminating the risks. There is always that tendency that things may go south, and you may lose out on your money.

6. Funds Investing

Funds investing or investment funds is one way to get to your dream of being a strategic investor. An investment fund is like a database. It is a combina tion of funds – a combined supply of capital – which is owned by and contributed to by a large number of investors. The goal of the money generated is to purchase securities and assets; but even after this is done, every investor retains ownership and control over his shares. Just like mutual and index funds, investment funds provide a greater array of investment opportunities for each of the investors; and as a result of this, it is a good way to pursue your dreams of financial freedom.

Investment funding comes with its own share of challenges, including those affiliated with index funding and mutual funding. The vast array of opportunities found here also imply that there is a vast array of dangers and risks to face. It is usually advisable to seek the help and advice of experts.

Usually, companies and government-owned organizations put out advertisements whenever they seek investors. When these calls go out, potential investors heed them, and depending on considered factors, decide whether they will take the plunge and invest in the company. If they invest, they do so with hopes that the climate in the marketplace is favorable. This does not rule out that there may be issues that arise, seeing as the investor market is volatile.

Depending on how well the investor did his homework and ensured that he was not set up to take the fall if things do not go well, he may make a good fortune out of his investments. When this happens, the Return on Investment (ROI) is high. Return on investment is the reward that comes from any investment – and it can either be bad or good. When ROI is low, it means that that venture may not be your best option.

There are many things to consider before making an investment. These are the rudimentary things that many people tend to overlook, and the result is that they get burned. When this happens, they tend to write off investments and say that they do not work. As someone who has been in the investment industry for a while, I can tell you that a huge quota of the investments which turn out wrong could be averted, if only the investors had studied what they were about to put their money into.

Here are the things you must consider before you make your next investment, unless you are looking to flush your money down the drain.

Things to Look Out for Before You Invest

1. Company Management

This is usually the first thing people are advised to look out for before they invest; and surprisingly, this is the one thing that many people overlook when they are about to make their investment decisions.

This is a no-brainer. A healthy company with a high ROI is built off the sweat, diligence, hard work, and discipline of a team of smart individuals. The team is put together by another team, known as the administrative body of the organization. It is safe to say that the health of an organization is determined by the sanity of its management.

One of the responsibilities of management is to make decisions that are in the best interest of the company. They achieve this by having the foresight to see what others are not seeing, plot and strategize their way around everything that can arise to cause holdups in the future, and take care of the tough decisions. The management of every firm keeps things in check and running smoothly.

But what happens when the management is dysfunctional? Your guess is as good as mine – there is bound to be a dysfunctional company.

There are a few questions you must ask yourself and be honest with the answers you give. Some of them include: how competent are the people at the top? Is the company innovative, and does it have what it takes to weather storms in the marketplace? What are the general culture and work ethics of the company?

It is necessary that you study the management of every company before you commit your money to an investment. If you invest in a company with bad management, chances are that you will lose out on this investment because any times, bad management is a precursor to a company closing down. If a company has bad management, which is reflected in bad choices over time and the overall deterioration of the company; it is in your best interest that you do not invest in it at all.

2. Company Stability

This is the first thing you must check, unless you are looking to dash your money away with no hopes of making it back. One thing wise investors always look out for is the stability of the company in the marketplace. This stability covers a lot of things, including:

- **Stability of company earnings** calculated over time.

- **Stability of management and the quality of decisions/actions taken by the company,** especially in the face of hard times in the market and industry.

- **Stability of investors, and the experiences they have with the company.** If the former investors have a track record of being satisfied with investing in the company' then it is an indication that you, too, will get the best out of your investment venture.

- **Stability of the marketplace, especially of the equities you want to invest in.** for example, investing in company stocks and bonds is a great way to accumulate wealth over time, and this can be achieved faster by compounding. But if your goal is to invest in the now and yield quantum results almost immediately, you may want to look at investing in other industries like digital currencies including forex, and other e-currencies.

The reason is that these markets are highly unstable, and within a matter of seconds, the prices of various elements can shoot across different areas of the money spectrum – literally. In this scenario, the person may stand the chance of making a lot of money, but the market is not too stable in terms of being predictable with outcomes.

When looking to invest in a company, make sure that the company has shown to be active and has gained stability. This is easier to obtain in the case of companies that achieve remarkable amounts of clout and notoriety in the marketplace. On the other hand, companies in the infancy stage can be traced, and you can make educated guesses based on a few indices. These indices include; the industry these companies are in, the management of these companies, the quality of products/services they offer, their strategies and the processes they have put in place to ensure that they do not go out of business, etc.

Company stability is one of the first things you must look out for before you commit your funds to any company. Any organization that is already stable and has gathered some amount of company clout is more likely to yield more results.

3. **Dividends**

   These are only available to investors in companies that have already gained a measure of stability. Smaller companies may not have what it takes to pay their investors dividends, and while you can overlook this, it is advisable that you get companies that are able to pay small dividends that increase over time.

   This is because, with the principle of compounding, you stand to gain much more in a company that has what it takes to pay dividends as time goes on. Inasmuch as it is advised to find and invest in companies that can pay dividends; also, please be careful of companies that promise to pay very high yields and dividends. Sometimes this may be a way to attract investors to a company that is on the verge of being sucked under the waves and declaring bankruptcy. Once this is the case, please do not invest.

4. **Financial Conditions of the Company**

   According to the U.S. Security Exchange Commission (SEC), public companies are mandated to make their financial reports available to the public.

These reports are a gross overview of the company's financial status and are available to the public, especially potential investors. The financial reports are a general peep into the company's finances, not an in-depth view of what the company's finances look like.

Before investing in a company, look at the company's financial status. With the knowledge you gain, you will be equipped to make the best and smartest decisions as to whether you will gain from the investments.

Here is a little litmus test to know whether a company is worth investing in.

Companies that shroud their financial reports too well, and at the same time promise too-high yields, are not the best option. This is because the financial reports give you insights into the company's earning capacity, and as we discussed earlier, the company's earning power gives you an idea into whether this company is going to appreciate with time. Because of this, it is vital that you examine the company's financial conditions – they may not be your idea of ideal, but there are a few things that can be red flags. Once you see these red flags, it is best you do not invest in those companies.

5. **Price of the Stocks/Bonds You Are to Buy**

    It is only smart to want to buy at a price that is reasonably lower than the investment will be sold. The price margin that exists between buying and selling prices can determine whether it is a great investment or not. As we discussed earlier, you buy at a lower price and sell at a higher price. With this knowledge in mind, look out for stocks, bonds, and equities that are cheaper than what they can be sold for, and which have the potentials to yield much more.

    If you are to buy at a rate that is exorbitant and exceedingly high, how then do you plan to make your money back?

6. **Company Assets vs Liabilities**

    This is another thing that many investors do not consider before putting their resources into a company or organization. A company that has more liabilities than assets is more likely to be a bad idea for investment. To be on the safer side, look to invest in companies that have at least double the amount of assets they have as liabilities.

Assets are those things that contribute to the progress of the company and help them achieve their money goals. Liabilities, on the other hand, take away from the overall value of the company, and this is the easiest recipe for company deterioration. When carrying out your studies, and you are about to invest, look for companies that have more assets than liabilities. It is also best you invest in companies that are debt-free, or that have more assets to swallow up the amount of debts they owe.

Taking the decision to be an investor in any company is a scary one. As a result of this, it is advisable that you carry out as much research as is possible. This way, you know exactly where you are about to put your money, and you also know the odds of success for the venture.

Inasmuch as there are options when it comes to investing, there are people in the market who are just looking to get a quick fix. These people are not in it for the long run. They are looking to invest in something today and make as much gain as they can.

These people are known as short-term investors, and there are a few ideas for them to make the most out of their expedition.

Here are a few short-term investment ideas if you are in this category.

Short-Term Investment Ideas

If you are looking to make a short-term investment, it is probably because you need some immediate financial help. You may be strapped for cash and in need of an immediate redemption, or you may be not cut out for the hassles associated with the investment world. In either case, you are in the right place, because as you read through the following, you will be exposed to a few ideas that can give you a quick win and set you up almost immediately.

First off, short-term investments are those you make for periods of time less than three years. The thing about short-term investments is that you sacrifice the benefits that accrue by making longer-term investments. As a result of the high rate of returns that are associated with short-term investing, it is not unusual for people to go for them at the mercy of the benefits that they can get from long-term investments.

However, here are the ideas that can help you attain your short-term investing goals.

1. **Savings Accounts**

    Savings accounts are a secure way to keep your money, and have it yield some level of returns. Savings accounts are controlled by banks and savings unions and are useful ways to make sure that the money you have put away keeps on increasing. Savings accounts pay a limited amount of money in return for keeping money with them.

    Consider these interests you receive for saving money with these institutions as the dividends you earn in bigger companies. The only differences are that what you receive as interest for putting your money away in a savings account is much smaller than what you will receive if you put that sum away in a long-term venture. Another difference is that the money you put in a savings account is easily accessible and is not tied down by time limitations. This implies that at any time the need arises, you can access your money, and this is not the case with investing in a longer-term scheme.

Before investing in savings accounts, compare banks and find out which have the best offers in terms of higher interest rates. When you find this, be sure to keep up with the issues that relate to money and finances in the economy. One of the reasons why people tend to put their money away in savings accounts is because there is really no risk attached to it. The only challenge is that as time unfolds, inflation can lead to changes in terms of how much they earn from keeping money in savings accounts.

2. **Short-Term Corporate Bond Funds**

These are bonds sold by major corporations to fund projects and keep up with the daily running of their businesses. Short-term corporate bonds are a great way to invest money now and get a return in a short while. As opposed to the normal three years and more it takes for bonds to mature, these investments begin to yield rewards at an early stage. These investments are typically considered safe, and they pay those that purchased them a reasonable amount of interest at regular intervals throughout the year.

Corporate bonds are an accumulation of many different bonds from different companies and corporate bodies, perhaps in different markets and industries. These bonds are from various organizations, and the risks are less when one bond does not perform as well as it should, because others can cover up for it. The red light when it comes to these bonds is that the government does not insure them. There is the risk that they can lose money at any time, and there is little or nothing that can be done.

Coupled with the fact that these do not pay as much as long-term bonds and other financial investments, tread with caution. These bonds are highly liquid, and they can be traded at any time the market is open.

3. **Money Market Accounts**

Consider these to be another form of savings accounts. The only major difference between the two is that this category usually pays higher interest, although the investment timeframe is still small. Normally, the investments are higher than what can be contained in the savings account; hence, this is usually cost-intensive.

If you are going to consider putting your money in

this venture, it is advisable that you find market accounts that are protected by FDIC insurance. This protects your investments from the threat of sudden dissolution, hence providing a semblance of comfort and security. One thing to note is that this kind of investment is most suited for the short-term, because as the amount of interest paid over time is little, investors find it difficult to keep up with inflation.

4. **Treasuries**

These come in a host of varieties – T-bills, T-bonds, and T-notes. They are backed up by the government's promises and intentions to pay back the money, so treasuries are safe, although they are not insured. This should be an issue, but it usually does not prove to be one because of the vocal promises the government makes once it allows the public to gain access to treasury funds.

Treasury bonds are highly liquid and can be sold on any day of transaction in the market. As a result, access to treasury bonds is not too difficult.

If you are looking to get started with any investment scheme, but at the same time seeking something that is not too long-term and involved as the ones that are discussed in earlier sections of this book, the few options outlined above are a great place to start. Just be sure to take a deeper look at them before you make a decision about one to get the highest return rate possible.

How to Make the Most of Your Investments

Although we looked at a vast array of investment options that you can cash in and make the right choices and build a portfolio for yourself, you must understand that there is a skill to investing. You do not do everything, anyhow, and expect that there will be great results. As a result of this knowledge, there are a few things you must know if you want to make the most of your investments.

1. Diversify Your Investments

This is a golden rule about investments. Diversify your investments. There is no one-cloak-fits-all approach when it comes to investing. If you have what it takes, try as many options as you can and see the different possibilities you can create as you make more progress in your investing journey.

So instead of focusing on one kind of investment, try

to spice it up by delving into some other investments in other industries. The goal is to make sure that you do not put all your eggs in one basket, and to do this, it is advised that you diversify. While diversifying, ensure that you combine different investment types. A safer way to go about this may be to try out investing in an index and mutual funds, and maybe also selecting one form of short-term investment to work on. Remember to take these on as much as you can, and do not invest in such a way that it becomes detrimental to your finances.

2. xxxxxxxx (needs title)

The type of investments you want to go into determines the approach you take. If you are about to go into investments that come in buckets – like index and mutual funds, and any other thing that necessitates an eye for details and keen attention – it is necessary to seek the help of experts.

These people have been in the industry for a while, and they understand the nitty-gritty of what it is you want to achieve. As a result of this, they are in a better position to ensure that you make guided decisions that yield the best of results as you go on in your investing journey. If, on the other hand, you are looking to invest in a short-term venture, it is advisable that you study extensively the types of short-term investments there are and make the most appropriate decisions. In any case, do not venture into investing if you do not understand the market and know how to navigate it properly.

3. **Understand Liquidity**

Liquidity is the ability of an asset to be sold at any time without the value of this asset being compromised. This can also mean this asset can easily be converted to cash. Before investing in any industry or asset, make sure that what you are investing in is liquid enough – especially if you know you are going to be cashing out of that investment in the short-run. If your assets are not liquid, you will be making a grave mistake and spending your money on things that will not give you good profits.

Key Points From This Chapter

This chapter examined the concept of basic investing and the different forms of investing.

1. The goal of investing is to get returns that are higher than whatever you have put in. To achieve, this there are a few things you must know.

2. Before investing, understand the types of investment schemes and work on building your investment portfolio. One of the best options is to invest in a lucrative asset or industry over time and allow your rewards to increase over time by compounding.

If you are looking to invest in assets that are a bit more complicated because they are made up of smaller assets, like mutual funds, it is necessary and advisable that you begin your journey consulting with a finance consultant or a specialist in investing. These people are your best bet because they are in the position of offering you advice that will help get you started on the right track.

If, on the other hand, you do not have what it takes to get these people in your corner, maybe because of financial and other logistic challenges, you can look at other low-risk investments. These include investing in stocks and bonds of corporate bodies that have achieved some level of stability in the marketplace or in those of government-owned organizations. You may also want to take a look at investing in short-term assets and industries, but be sure to conduct your market research well so that you know what to do and how to go about it.

3

ASSETS IN YOUR PORTFOLIO: WHY DO THEY MATTER?

In the previous chapter, we introduced the concept of assets as it relates to investing, and we also talked about how you can start building an irresistible portfolio. In this chapter, we take that conversation a step further.

I began to understand the value of investments and building a portfolio as I began to grow older. I discovered that it was not common for a person to talk about building wealth in the ghetto; talk more about getting a portfolio of investments that can afford you and your family the luxury of being financially independent. The result is that people who grew up around me did not know that it was possible to become financially free and build up an investment portfolio that is good enough to gain financial independence and last generations to come.

As I began to dabble into investing, I learned that the value of an investment portfolio is too much, and cannot and should not be ignored by anyone who wants to journey into the world of investing. First things first, let us begin from the beginning.

What is an Investment Portfolio?

An investment portfolio is a collection of individual investments, such as stocks, bonds, cash, and other forms of investments. This is one of the most proven ways of investing, and investors ensure that they gather as many investment units as they can into their portfolio. The reasons for this include:

- A wider portfolio shows that the person has a wider understanding of the investment market. This is especially useful for those who plan to be investment tutors and experts to guide people on their investment journeys.

- The wider the portfolio, the fewer risks associated with it. When an investor is in possession of a wide portfolio of investments, he is immune from sudden and unprecedented changes in the marketplace. This is because one change cannot drastically affect all other assets. As a result, other assets may cover for one case of something ugly.

- The more assets in your portfolio, the more the interest and profit you can potentially make, especially if you are guided by an expert.

When you get older and have more responsibilities, you begin to see the benefits of having a stream of investments and assets in your portfolio, because they serve to get you closer to your dream of gaining financial independence. In this chapter, we talk about these individual investments that make up your portfolio; and how you can take specific assets and develop them into a portfolio and allow the principle of compounding do the thing it can do best.

Different types of investments to add to your portfolio.

There are a few investment options you can add to your portfolio.

1. REIT (Real Estate Investment Trust).

These are managed by major corporations and industries that offer real estate solutions to a wide clientele. Simply put, REITs are real estate and a mortgage-free life on a budget.

Over the years, REITs have proven to be one of the most sought-after investment opportunities. This is because real estate on its own is seen as a real-time asset; and land as we know, does not depreciate. Statistics show that real estate, as a sector of the investment industry, it has produced a lot of millionaires. This is because of the low risk involved, and the fact that real estate is highly valuable. Real estate hardly depreciates, so it is a great place to start your investing venture.

REITs are amazing because they have various plans for various classes of people. Even if you do not have what it takes to buy a landed property or clear up the mortgage on a property upfront, some REITs allow you to buy real estate exposure without physically buying real estate. Another reason why a REIT is a great place to start is that it yields profits like bonds; and as a result, the owner has access to interest on a regular basis – sometimes quarterly, sometimes annually.

A single REIT covers a range of real estate property. A good investor knows that this is fodder for more, because no real estate investor refuses the prospect of more avenues to invest and increase earnings. One thing many real estate investors do not know is that there are many more ways to make profits from investing in real estate than just buying a landed property.

Other investment opportunities in real estate include property management, renting out the property, and the generic buying and selling of property. In any case, there is a lot that can be made from real estate; and you need to be a keen investor to make the most out of your decision to invest in real estate.

If you make the most of investing in REITs, you must know the various forms of REITs that exist and how each of these plays a part in the actualization of your financial goals. Here is a rundown of these.

A. Retail REIT. These cover shopping malls, strip malls, and free-standing shopping centers. This type of REIT is based on the belief that shopping malls clout and can generate the amount of money needed to keep the investment profitable. Retail REITs are usually easier to get started with and are a great source of income, especially if invested in wisely.

B. Residential REITS. As the name implies, this has to do with residential apartments and live-in quarters for individuals. This includes options like apartments, single-family homes, and other facilities that have the same functionalities – that are built with the sole purpose of having people inhabit them. This, in the opinion of many major investors, is one way to invest wisely in real estate.

1. Health REITs. These cover an important aspect of man's living – health and health facilities. When you choose to invest in health REITs, you are choosing to invest in properties like hospitals, medical centers, old peoples' homes/senior housing centers, and all the rest of them. Investing in these is also a great choice because hospitals and medical centers bring in a good amount of money over time.

2. Safe choice REITs. These are those kinds of REITs that cover houses and facilities that are strictly used for business purposes, especially on a large scale. These include factories, warehouses, depots, and other large facilities.

3. The last type of REITs covers mutually used spaces like small motels, big-size hotels, and everything in-between. These are beneficial because they are usually buildings used for commercial purposes and have a wide stream of clientele and people that frequent them.

They are a great place to invest your money, if you are looking for relatively safer places to avoid a lot of casualties.

With the right research, you will see that you have the best kind of REIT to invest in and get enough ROI; and over time, following the principle of compounding, you will be able to make much more from your initial investment. REITs are a great way to start building your portfolio so that, in no time, you can see returns, which only increase with time. Here's another thing about these types of investments that make them a great option for investing; 90 percent of the profits from these investments go to the shareholder, while the remaining 10 percent are recycled back to the company. This is law ensures that the shareholder gets the most he can get from his money, while still ensuring that the company never runs out. Considering this, and the fact that real estate has the potential for high turnover in finances, total profit options are limitless, especially for the person who figures out the best place to invest.

4. Bond Investing.

Bond investing is the practice of buying bonds from major corporations and business outfits with the sole intent of making profits when there is a need for these bonds to be sold. This is the scenario that plays out whenever you are to buy bonds:

A bond is a fixed-income investment that the bond issuer (the company who wishes to sell bonds with which they can get money to finance projects and do everything in-between) borrows money from an investor (the individual willing to buy over these bonds at a predetermined price). The investor receives the bonds, and under the promise of keeping to a schedule, interest payments known as coupons are issued to him regularly. These coupons are a means to incentivize him and thank him for allowing the use of his money. As these are issued, a date when the full amount of money he borrowed will be paid back in full (maturity date) is promised him.

Bonds can be issued by different companies and government-owned agencies. For example, the U.S. government issues bonds to citizens. These are known as treasury bonds or sovereign bonds. The governments of states also have bonds they issue to citizens of their states. These are Municipal bonds. There is one good thing about municipal bonds, and this is what many people who know about them seek. When you are issued a municipal bond, state taxes and rates are deducted. This implies that the state can levy your taxes and other state-inclined bills you are obligated to pay when you are a possessor of bonds in the state. Many people consider bonds as an easy way to pay up their debts on a budget.

There are two major kinds of bonds that you should be aware of.

The first is zero coupon bonds. These bonds are issued at a discount and mature at full value. During the course of the lifetime of this bond's transaction, the investor is entitled to small amounts of coupons, and sometimes he may not even get one. These bonds usually only pay off by the expiration of the bond; and just like every other bond, their pay-off and ROIs can be impressive.

Another type is convertible bonds. These are fluid bonds, and can be converted into common stock at any point. The major privileges attached to these bonds include their ability to be converted into stocks on specific terms, redeemable at specific times of the year.

This is where many people who want to invest in stocks and bonds make a major mistake. They think that they must spend all their money to find a stock that is reasonably priced and does not come with a lot of conditions. Every stock/bond you can invest in comes with its own share of conditions that you must make informed decisions about and sometimes trust your instincts; it is best to note that there are certain bonds that can allow you the luxury of having certain benefits. These benefits include more ROI and generally being in a position to make more money from these bonds. It is wise that you spend time doing your research before you commit your finances and resources to any bonds. There are bond agencies that can help you make informed decisions so that you can make the most out of your investments.

There are different classes of bonds you can invest in. All three classes have their peculiarities and what makes them ideal for specific people.

The first kind is investment-grade bonds. These are the best of the best bonds. They are cost-intensive to purchase; and if left to grow by compounding, they have the most turnover. In this category, triple A bonds are the best, and they perform the best.

The other kind is junk bonds. As the name implies, these are not as good as the investor category in terms of turnover. They are moderate-to-low in terms of the investment and ROI. As they are not as great as investment-grade bonds, these are also a great way to start on your journey to financial freedom. These bonds come with a lot of investments like stocks, money market accounts, and all the rest of them.

Asset Allocation

Now that we have looked at the different investments to add to your portfolio, it is vital that we also look at asset allocations. These serve to provide a balance for us to work with. People make grave mistakes because they do not understand that you need to balance your allocations in such a way that you do not put all eggs in one basket.

In the last chapter, we discussed how it is in your best interest for you to diversify your investments. This way, you can make more profits and ensure that you get more returns, as time goes on.

Asset allocation is the name given to the word – balance – in the investment sector. It ensures that all your assets and investments are balanced in such a way that you can diversify your income and earnings. A healthy asset allocation consists of assets including stocks of companies in various industries, bonds, and every other asset type you can think of.

Although it is a great idea to have your stocks and investments balanced, there are a few things you should note before you venture into these investments. If you are going to diversify your investments and make the most of this exercise, these are the things you must consider:

Things you must consider before venturing into this aspect of investment:

1. Your goals. The questions you must ask include why you are investing? The reason for investing determines the mode of investments that you take, how much of your energies you are going to channel into it, and the exact investments you make.

If you are investing to gain financial help in the near future, you know the exact investments to venture into. This is how knowing exactly what you want to achieve with your investments helps you make wise choices.

2. You must consider your risk tolerance level. We established that all investment schemes have risk factors attached to them, but some are more risk-prone than others. If you are looking for a safe place to invest your money, especially in the short run, then there are places it is not advisable for you to invest.

If you are this person, buying stocks from a new com

pany that is yet to achieve stability in the marketplace may not be the smartest move because the nature of the company, and the fact that it is yet to gain notoriety in the marketplace, may indicate you may not be getting your money back immediately. We are not going to rule out the fact that anything can happen to your investment in a company in its infancy stages. A more appropriate move may be government-owned treasury bills, or at least getting a savings account in a bank that pays a reasonable amount as interest.

3. Liquidity of your investments. It is more appropriate for you to invest in assets that are more liquid and can easily convert to cash. This enabled you to make the transitions and switch back to cash immediately, should the need arise. Because of this, spend time finding out exactly what kind of assets you want to invest in; and how feasible it is for you to get them.

4. Variety. The goal of asset allocation is to make sure that you have a variety of investments in your portfolio. When allocating your assets, make sure you purchase as many asset types as you can from different companies in different industries. This enables you to hit your financial goals faster than if you put all your eggs in one basket. Also, if you practice this, you wouldn't be setting yourself up for a major fall if something happens to one of your investment buckets.

Asset Classes

If you have gotten this far into the book, congratulations.

The reason for that is because you most likely are looking to invest, and that is a great decision. In this section, we discuss asset classes and what they mean to your portfolio.

First off, an asset is a group of investment options or financial securities that exhibit the same characteristics and are bound together by the same set of regulative laws.

1. Equities (stocks/securities). These assets go by a number of names. This part of your portfolio has unlimited potential and can grow into unprecedented wealth if you make the right selections, and you have a great financial investment expert to guide you. This is the most liquid asset class; and if left to compound, they can yield the most in terms of ROI.

2. Fixed-income bonds. These are high-converting investment schemes that pay a fixed amount of interest to the investors in form of coupons. If you purchase a fixed-income bond, for the period of time the contract is legally valid, you are entitled to receive a commission of interests in form of coupons. These coupons have different monetary values and are given as the company's way of appreciating investors while ensuring that they do not go out of business. These coupons and other associated payments are usually delivered at specific times of the year; and at the end of the agreement (maturity time), the money that is invested is returned to the investors.

3. Cash and cash equivalent options. These are investment securities designed to benefit the investor in the short run. These are investment odds that are highly lucrative in that they yield a handsome ROI almost immediately after investment.

These investments are low risk, and with respect to what can be earned over time, they pale in comparison. These include treasury bills, corporate commercial papers, and other relevant bank documents.

In order to make the best choices, be sure to go through the details that are conveyed in this chapter and ensure that you adhere strictly to what you learned. If you are in need of more help, reach out to a financial expert, because investing is like trying to read the weather; you have to be into a place and within a context to make the most out of it. As a result, do not be swift to invest, rather make sure you do your homework so as to avoid making a great mistake.

Key Points From This Chapter

1. Having an asset portfolio is one sure way to get out of poverty and into the place of financial freedom.

2. An asset portfolio gives you the advantage of being able to invest wider, make more money, and shield you from making sudden losses as you invest. This is due to the diversity in your portfolio. When one thing fails, the next thing can pick up to cover for it.

3. Before committing yourself to invest in any asset/financial security, make sure you understand it well. This way, you can able make the best decisions and not shoot yourself in the foot.

4. Some assets are better if you invest in them and leave them to grow over the years, while others are not that suitable. Understand the nuances of every investment before you venture into it.

4

TIME MANAGEMENT AND PRODUCTIVITY HACKS

You may probably be asking yourself, why?

Why is the author talking about time management in a book that is centered on investing and investment schemes? Why not go straight to the point? Here is the thing. Time management and being productive is an inherent part of being a good investor. Every great investor knows this; you cannot be a good investor and make a good living for yourself and your family, and possibly generations to come, if you do not know how to be productive with every minute and how to make sure you are on top of your game when it comes to time management.

The reason for that is this: timing is everything.

Even the market you are about to invest in runs on timing, and it matters how you see time and the value you place on it.

So, to be a good investor, you must understand the sanctity of timing; and how you can make the most out of every second, especially regarding your life as an investor. In this chapter, we look at this concept. Here is a warning for you, though. This book does not center on timing and time management, so the knowledge you get from this chapter is not immersive and all-encompassing. Nevertheless, it is sufficient to start you on the right track and help set things in perspective.

Statistics show that the average human gets to live for an average of 675,450 hours. This seems like a long time, until you look back and see that you have been alive for 675,452 hours and still counting. At this point, the question becomes "where did all the time go?" People wake up and go about their lives without paying attention to the one thing that was given equally to all men by the one who created man.

Every man is not made and born equal. Banish the

thought that every man is equal. While it may be true on some level, the reality of life remains that not all men are equal. Some are wealthier. Some are more exposed. Some are more knowledgeable than others. Some seem to have it all, while others are left to dangle at the bottom of the food chain. Whatever the case is, many times, humans fixate so much on where they are different and what they do not have enough of that they forget the one thing that was given equally to everyone.

TIME!!!

The thing is, we fail to recognize that time is the gift we are given equally, and that it is up to each and every one of us to make the most out of our time.

Now, here's the sad thing about time. Time does not stop moving. Whether you spend the day snoozing on the couch or decide to go after the things you so desperately love and want to achieve does not change the fact that the hands of the clock are still ticking.

The bad news is that sooner or later, those 675,450 hours will be up. At the end, you may still be living, but it is not as it used to be when you were much younger with youth and the blessings of grace and strength on your side.

This is an imminent challenge to me and the number of people I have seen and helped conquer this challenge. Many investors, and those I have helped to get over the initial fear of investing and get on the boat fully, ask this question: I know there is so much I can achieve, but I cannot do as much as I want to do. How do I go about it?

Well, if you are asking that question, you are in luck. In this chapter, we do justice to it and provide you with helpful tricks and hacks to start you on the right track.

Ready?

What is Time Management?

Time management is the practice and principle of carefully allocating your time to everything you must do on a daily basis, setting up structures in your life that ensure you stay on top of your productivity game, and seeing that you follow to the letter all that you set out to do.

Many people do not understand that time management is more than a decision to be better and cram up your day full of activities; time management is action. It lies in your ability to say "NO" at some times, and say "YES" at other times. It lies in your ability to make decisions on what to do with days, and seeing it through until you complete everything on your list.

Time management is painful to the body. Time management is hard work, and this is because it takes a lot of discipline to manage your time.

I am about to share principles I use in my life to scale my productivity and make sure that I remain on top of my game as an investor, and a man with a full and busy life to live. Many other investors, successful business and career people, use these; and they increase their productivity levels and become better with time management.

Here are a few of these handy hacks we are talking about.

Productivity hacks to keep you on top of your game.

1. Start at the beginning; get a decent amount of sleep. The truth is that you can't achieve a lot if your brain is crowded and you feel tired as hell. You must determine exactly how much sleep you need to be productive and do your best to get it. Here's a quick one: there is a thin line that exists between getting just enough sleep and becoming lazy/procrastinating. Find that line, and make sure you do not start slipping over to the other side of the pendulum – laziness. In my opinion, if you sleep for 10-12 hours, you are losing precious hours of work. If you sleep for 6-8 hours, that may be okay.

The bottom line is to find that balance, and make sure you do not over-indulge yourself, especially if you have goals to work on.

2. Learn to FOCUS. Many times, we end up not being as productive as we can and know we should be, because we have not learned the subtle act of being focused. It is simple. FOCUS: Follow One Course Until Successful.

If you do not have focus, you will do everything, or try to do everything, only to discover that you have successfully done nothing. This is the key to becoming more successful and being a master.

3. Pre-plan your day. You cannot afford to live your day off the fly and expect to be highly productive and successful to boot. If there is one thing I have discovered, it is that successful people master the art of being productive, and they achieve this by planning out their day.

I advise that you start every day with a to-do list. It is a simple routine that helps me. Make a list of the things you want to get done and categorize the items based on how much of a priority they are to you and the actualization of your goals. This is to discipline yourself to focus on the tasks that are relevant to you and the actualization of your goals. Work your way down this list every day, and you will notice that you are becoming more productive.

4. Learn to manipulate time to work for you. Set alarms, reminders, and everything in-between that can remind you of the tasks you must achieve. Once you do this, you are on your way to living a more productive life.

You must be able to make to interject work hours with hours of rest. Learn to space out your work and add in some rest between. Say you work for one hour, then take a few minutes off to rest and cool off your mind. This way, you get yourself into a state where you are more productive in the long run. Your brain does not want to be overwhelmed; do not overwhelm it with too much work.

5. Batch your tasks. If you have tasks that are the same or fall into the same category, you can take them up and carry them out at the same time. For instance, batch checking of e-mails at 4 p.m. This means that at 4 p.m., you sort through your mail, and make sure to leave nothing behind. This way, you do not walk around the whole day feeling that you are forgetting something.

6. Outwork your competition in the market. Remember, you are going into a field that is highly competitive – the investment sector. You must roll up your sleeves and get to work, even when no one sees you. This is what qualifies you to make it big in any field – the work you put in. Do not be too lazy to go for what you want. We have already been guided well in the last chapters to know that there are many things that do not come to you because you wish for them. You must go for them, and they will not come easy.

7. Put a monetary peg on your time. Many times, we waste time because we have not yet trained ourselves to see the value of time. Imagine you place a dollar against each minute of the day, and you decide you are going to be working for seven hours every day. This means that if you waste half an hour of that time, you have lost $30. Who likes to lose money unnecessarily?

Definitely not you, I guess…

Put all these hacks to mind and remember that your time is one of the most valuable currencies you have. If you fail to make the most of it, you will reach the pinnacle of your career and the things you can achieve as you move on.

Key Points From This Chapter

1. There is only one thing that everyone has equal, and that thing is time.

2. We all have 24 hours in a day, but it is up to us to decide how we want to spend every second. If we waste time on activities that are not profitable, we end our lives without living to the fullest. This is one recipe for a disastrous life.

3. Even as a potential investor, learn the value of time. The market you are about to invest in runs on timing, and you will make a grave mistake to not pay attention to how you spend each hour of your day.

4. If you are looking for hacks to make you stay productive and get more out of every second of your day, look at the minimized list given above. That list gives you action points.

5

CREATING A BUSINESS OR INVESTING IN YOUR NICHE: WHICH ONE IS A BETTER OPTION FOR YOU?

During the course of my career as an investment expert, I have come across a lot of young men who do not know whether it is better for them to create a business, or what next steps they must take.

Here's the scenario:

You have been told that you are good at something. Maybe it is something you have never seen as a big deal before now, but you see that it is something that people have a need for, and they seem to idolize you when you do that one thing. At first, you never took them seriously, but when the compliments began to increase, you felt those compliments slip through the cracks that were forming in your brain.

You are between worlds; you do not know whether it is best for you to keep playing it safe, or if you should venture into the deep and become an entrepreneur. Well, in this chapter, you get some clarity on what you must do next.

First things first; you may not need a college degree if you want to become an entrepreneur and build yourself a thriving business. This may be a relief to you if you do not have a degree. But whether or not you have a degree, you must have the drive, passion, and courage to be an entrepreneur. This is not a walk in the park; and if you do not learn this now, you are buttering yourself up for a heart break. So, if you want to start a business, here are a few actionable steps you can take:

Things You Should do in Preparation to be an Entrepreneur

1. Your research.

So, you have decided to be an entrepreneur, right? The truth of this is that you will not make a lot of progress if you venture into business and being an entrepreneur without carrying out your research and doing it well. Have you ever wanted to go on an expedition to a place you have never been, maybe the heart of the safari? The first thing you do is pull out your device and search on Google what the safari looks like. You look at the things that thrive there, the animals that live in the safari, and their lifestyles. This knowledge equips you to know exactly what to expect there, and how to weather storms and the challenges that come from there.

If you do this with a trip, why wouldn't you do it with a venture as big as this one? Many people venture into business, and they give little or no thought to the research they should do before starting. The result is that they gas out as fast as they went into that venture. Before starting a business, evaluate yourself. Ask and answer pertinent questions like:

- Who am I? (Your identity matters a lot in business, and it is vital because it helps you build self-confidence, which is something you need to thrive as an entrepreneur).

- What is my aim for starting up this business? (The answer to this question helps you not make a mistake. Many people venture into business with hopes that it will be a fix-it-quick scheme for all their money issues. If you are looking for something that can give you fast cash today, you may need to go and get a job, because business can take time before you begin to see the results.

- What solutions am I offering in the marketplace? (This helps you know if that is a viable business idea or not).

- Who am I offering these solutions to? (This helps you know who you are targeting; and you, therefore, put strategies on the ground to ensure that you make the most out of your business venture).

- What is my customer avatar? (This is where you begin to make an educated guess as to the various characteristics of your ideal client. Take note of their likes and dislikes and what they want that will make them in the market and in search of your products. These questions begin to give you an idea of who these people are, and how you can best position your business to be seen, heard, and become the delight of them all. If you do not carry out this step, you are in for a rough ride; because you are creating products and offering services that are not needed by the people you are looking to attract. As a result, you will soon be frustrated out of business).

- Is there a need for the value I am offering in the marketplace? (This way you know whether it is a great idea or not).

- What is (are) my temperaments? (As infinitesimal and unrelated to business as this looks, it plays a major role in determining the kind of business you venture into; and how you begin to delegate duties, responsibilities, and roles in the hierarchy of your organization).

- Are my business ideas relatable? (Some ideas sound too good in your head – and honestly, that is where they should remain, in the head.) Before you begin any business-founding venture, find a trusted person(s) and talk to them about your business ideas and listen to what they have to say. You will be surprised at what you will find out).

- What do I know about the business I want to venture into? This helps you put things in perspective.

Moving on, as you conduct your research, you may want to take a deep look at the industry you are planning to go into. Study in the industry and find out how your potential clients and competition respond in time with the competition. Your research must also cover the business models and strategies of successful outlets in your industry, and you will find ways to adapt these to what you do at every stage of your business.

2. Decide what your company will be called. This is

helpful as you look at incorporating your business and make it an official and legally recognized entity.

3. **Decide on your business structure.** Will your business be a(n):

> **A. Sole-proprietorship.** In this, you hold most or all the powers, and you control your business as you see fit.
>
> **B. LLC.** A Limited Liability Company allows you to purchase insurance. The owners are responsible for debts only to the amount of investments they have put in. According to Wikipedia, this business structure combines the pass-through taxation of a partnership or sole proprietorship with the limited liability of a corporation. This implies there are a number of owners and investors, and they all come together to establish their outfit. The goal is to surmount challenges that may arise while creating the business, and also to make sure that more resources are made available.
>
> One business that chooses this model is made-to-grow companies. These companies usually start out on a smaller scale; and over time, as a result of

collective efforts, they expand to what the owners envisioned.

4. Now that you have all these details fleshed out, it is high time your business registered with the government. This one step is a sign that you want to take the plunge and make sure that you are a legalized entity. The laws that guide the registration of businesses may vary across states, but they end up at the same point. The baseline is an incorporated business, and when you have done this, you get an Employee Identification Number (EIN). You can then open a business account, which is a helpful way to ensure that you separate your personal money from business funds.

5. If your business is a service-based business, you want to make sure that you have the service permits that are issued by the appropriate bodies. These are necessary to ensure that you can serve people and do not lose out on your business when the chips are down. The next box you need to check is the insurance box. Are there bills you need to pay as a business owner to run your business on a full-scale? Please find all those bills and pay them.

No one likes the effects that come from the compounding of bills, especially if they could have been avoided in the first place. Make sure you pay off all your bills and ensure your business. No one knows what can happen. We are not trying to be negative here. It is just a fact.

Ensure your business with the proper insurance corporations.

6. Where is your business located? If you are looking to position your business for massive hits and a lot of profits, you must put this into consideration. You do not want to set up a physical business or a product-based business in the heart of nowhere, and in a place where the people who need your products do not have easy access to them. This is counter-productive. Try to avoid it.

Another thing you need to consider is how accessible your business is. Inasmuch as you may not be dealing in digital products and online things, you need to position your business in such a way that people know that you are reachable, especially whenever they want to do business with you. This is one way that you can make more profits and also ensure that you do not leave money on the table – by making sure that your business has an online handle that is active and can be found on the web.

7. Another check box you must tick off is funding. Many entrepreneurs fail to figure their businesses out. Who is funding this business? How do I get the money that to make sure that I can keep up with the daily activities of my business? To answer this question, you must look at the capital you have at hand – and by capital, I am talking about human and other kinds of capital, including money.

At this stage, begin brainstorming ideas through which you can set up your business. Will you seek the help of external investors, or will you fund the business yourself? At what point will you seek investors to put funds in the business? At the infancy stage or at the growth stage? When you have figured these out, you need to decide exactly how you will attract investors, if they are a part of your plan. What investment packages can your business put out to the public to attract the attention of the people you want to invest in your business? When you can answer these questions and more, you begin to see clearly how you can position your business to attract the funds that are needed to grow.

If you do not have a lot of options for funding, you can begin by writing out a strong business plan, and sending it off to banks and other financial houses to see if they can help you with a loan. You can send that off to bigger corporations who may be interested in funding your business. With the right strategies, you will find the best funding option for your business.

While it is difficult to make the transition to becoming an entrepreneur because of the risks associated and the uncertainties that are scattered all the way to your journey, it is vital that you get off on your best foot. If you are looking to open a business, become known over time, get paid for being a business owner, and remain in business for as long as you can (and even longer than you can imagine); then you must make sure that you put your best foot forward from the beginning and become the leading person in the field.

The truth about business is that there are certain people who you can't do business with, and there are some heights you cannot attain until you learn that you must do your homework well. So, as you journey to becoming an entrepreneur, remember that it is a long and sometimes arduous journey, but the end will usually justify the path you have walked.

Key Points From This Chapter

1. We cannot rule away from the fact that the journey to entrepreneurship is a long, hard, and sometimes arduous journey. You must determine to take it seriously and give it your best shot.

2. Not everyone is cut out to be an entrepreneur. Some people do much better if they can be true to themselves and find out what they are cut out to do. This way, they do not end up starting something they will not complete.

3. Before you start out on your entrepreneurship journey, be sure that you have done all you can to put your best foot forward. Revisit that section of the chapter where action points are given and begin your assignment from there. Work through the chapter and tick off boxes as you go.

6

BUDGETING FOR YOUR BUSINESS GOALS

In previous chapters of this book, we discussed at length the concept of investing, what it means to someone who is looking to start out, and how you can start setting up a business.

If you are to go off the knowledge you have gained so far, it would not be so bad. But for the sake of context, and also considering the fact that we started the journey to how you can get started with building a business, it is vital that we discuss this – because it is also a major part of running a successful business.

The concept of budgeting is one that has been highly

buttressed over the years, and sometimes, for all the wrong reasons. To some people, there is no need for a budget. For them, life is mostly spontaneous, and they can afford to do things off the fly. These are the people who have what it takes to step out from the house in the morning and just off a whim, make a detour to the nearest clothes store and spend the evening on a shopping spree. They end up driving back to the house at night, with their car trunks full of bags from various stores and outlets across town – outlets that are all too glad to have them visit again.

On the other hand, there are people who cringe at the thought of not living by and off a budget. To them, it is a nightmare to purchase a handkerchief that was not clearly stated in the budget for the month it will be purchased. These guys take pride in the fact that they have it all planned and figured down to a T. As a result of their little (or dare we say, massive) fixation on budgeting, they can hardly let their hair down and live a little.

In either case, these people may be at a loss for what they can possibly achieve. For the former category of people, they may get so spontaneous that they can spend any and everything that comes their way. This can become a challenge, because they do not know how to draw lines in the sand in such a way that it is clear. On the other hand, the latter category of people may just be too rigid for their own good. This rigidity can be both great and not-so-cool. It can be great because they would have known how well they can manage themselves and stick to a financial plan. On the other hand, it can be a bit challenging, if not detrimental to them to because they may just pass on an offer and opportunity, and just because they did not budget for it, they may end up losing out.

So, you see? Being on either end of the spectrum may not be the best option for you as a business owner who wants to be the best at what he does. Because of this, and the knowledge that finances are an inherent part of running a successful business, in this chapter we throw a little more light on the concept of budgeting and raising funds.

Having a great business idea or experiencing that eureka moment is only half the battle. It is only the smaller half of the battle. The challenge is that entrepreneurs, and those that have a business idea, often settle for enjoying how the whole thing plays out in their minds. So, he may spend the entire night thinking about how amazing it is to be that dream boss he wants to be, sitting at the helm of affairs of a multimillion-dollar business with international extensions and alliances. The thing is this fantasy only lasts for as long as it can. Sooner or later, he is bound to get off that high and come back to face his reality.

As a result of how daunting it gets – that is the quest to raise enough money to start your business with – many entrepreneurs give up and do not see it through until the end. In this chapter, we throw some light on a few ways you can get the money to start your business.

How to Generate Funds for Your Business Without Breaking the Bank and Work on a Budget

Here are some easier and less-complicated methods and strategies you can begin applying now.

1. Ask friends, family, and people you know for a loan. This is assuming that you do not have enough money to invest in your business; because if you did, then you would not be looking for some extra cash. One of the easiest options is to start asking your friends, family, and the people you know to help.

Note that this is different from investor-sourcing. In this context, you are getting money from people that you know; and they also know that you will pay them back soon enough. The goal of this is to provide you with immediate cash for sponsoring your business.

2. You can also get loans, but from banks or other financial houses and institutions. Try as much as possible not to do this until you have exhausted your options.

3. In the process of starting out your business, and getting it off its feet, you will have to bootstrap. Bootstrapping is a fancy term that is given to the concept that you are doing a lot of the work on your own. Because you do not yet have the financial power, the strength, and what it takes to outsource many things, you may need to do a lot by yourself.

Adjusting to this takes a lot from you, and it demands that you end up trying to learn a lot, do a lot, and bridge gaps that should be filled by others. Remember, you are a start-up entrepreneur; and with time, you will have the needed resources to delegate jobs and tasks to other people. But until then, you may just have to adopt this as a process that can get you to remain on a budget. Bootstrapping also implies that you resort to making use of low-cost techniques to drive clout and traction. For example, you may need to make the most out of organic advertising if you do not have what it takes to undergo a traditional advertising or digital advertising campaign.

4. If you need some major funding, and you do not know exactly what to do, then you may need to look for investors. To get the attention of these people, get a solid business plan and have a strategy to launch it in such a way that potential investors see your business as a viable place to put in their money. Also, try getting the attention of a venture capitalist who can invest in your business – solo. To achieve this, you will allow the venture capitalist to have access to equities. This implies that he owns a part of your business; and, at the end of the day, you are seen to be as business partners.

5. Seek out angel investors. Although these are rare and difficult to find, it goes without saying that you can try searching for them. Angel investors are investors, but they invest in your business with no intents of getting anything out of it for themselves. Their passion and drive is to see you grow and make the most out of your ventures. This is why it is not easy to find these people.

6. You can also try to get the public to be a part of your money-raising venture by trying out crowdfunding. Crowdfunding is a system of raising huge sums of money by getting a reasonable amount of people to contribute. You can possibly raise any amount of money in record time; and you do not have to think about repaying because this is done out of free will and is seen as a gift of charity, although you should give some kind of reward to those who fund your business.

If you have been stuck at a place and trying to crack this code of raising money for your venture, try these out, and you will marvel at the wonders you will see happening for you.

Key Points From This Chapter

1. It is possible for you to fund your business, even as a start-up entrepreneur, without having to break the bank or kill yourself with worry.

2. There are different ways to achieve this. Try out these and lookout for more. Do not let lack of funds keep you from being as awesome as you can be and living out that dream of starting that business.

7

CEO MIND-SET

Over the years, as I grow in business and have the opportunity to meet with and connect to many entrepreneurs and budding entrepreneurs, I have come to discover one staggering thing about entrepreneurs.

Many entrepreneurs, especially budding entrepreneurs, celebrate being entrepreneurs a bit too much. They place so much emphasis on the paparazzi that comes with being the leader of a thriving business that is raking in the green notes on a daily basis. When they look up and see notable figures in the business and investment industries who have done well over the years, they seem to drool and have fantasies that they will someday be like us.

Once they take this look at us, the first things they see are the well-tailored-to-form suits worn on fit bodies whose feet have been covered in properly made and glossed-over shoes. They see leather wallets stashed full of dollar bills as they protrude out of back pockets. They see elegance, class, fame, and everything in-between. They see these, but they do not see the main things that they need to see – at least at their stage in business.

They do not see when that idea that morphed to become a billion-dollar idea today was formed in the depths of our minds. They do not see the hurt we faced, the hurdles we scaled, the many opportunities we had to pass, and whatnot. They do not see the battles we fought and won, especially the battle of the mind. They do not see these, and that is where they make a grave mistake.

Have you ever heard the saying that it all starts and ends in the mind? Have you ever heard that the mind is man's greatest asset and whosoever has a fully functional mind has a shot at greatness, no matter the odds? Have you heard that your mind is the powerhouse of your life, and that you are vested with the responsibility of guarding it like a sentry? Have you?

The great author and writer Napoleon Hill once wrote a

book that is a bestseller forever known as Think and Grow Rich. In this book, he takes time to stress the role of the mind in every aspect of man's life. The truth is this is no gibberish. The first step you must take if you are to be successful is to get your mindset right. Once you do this, and you can align yourself to the flow of greater good, you will be surprised at what you find that starts happening in your life and business.

As a CEO or the owner of a business, you must know that more is demanded of you; and you must be able to show some level of responsibility and duty towards the things you have mapped out to do and to become. As a CEO, you must be able to rise above the noise and the distractions that come from being around people in a fast-paced world. The term CEO is not just a title, it is a responsibility. It is a call for you to take over the reins of your life and business and be sure that you are driving the train where you want it to be. As a CEO, the first thing you must do to be successful is get your mindset right, and do away with limiting and overbearing beliefs because these are detrimental to your journey.

Here are a few mindset hacks that can help you position yourself and your business for more.

1. Ditch impostor syndrome. Impostor syndrome is

that little voice that you do not know lives in you but has a sadly accurate timing. It is that voice that sounds suspiciously like you talking to yourself, but the only thing is that it constantly tells you that you are not worth it and that you are a fraudster. This is the mindset that makes people short-change themselves and consciously step away from the spotlight, thereby keeping themselves and everything about them small and mediocre.

If you are going to do and become more as an entrepreneur, blaze more trails, and perform giant strides, you must ditch imposter syndrome by constantly reminding yourself that you are worth it. You must tell yourself that you are capable and well-equipped for the job at hand, and that you will stop making it look as if you are the worst amongst your competition. This is not modesty. It actually eats you up from within and tanks your productivity.

2. Stop giving excuses. Excuses are a lazy man's apology, right? This is one of the major reasons why many CEOs and businesses never go as far as they could. If you keep making room for excuses, you will always see them; and this means that you will not be able to get anything worthwhile done. Next time you are facing a huge task, and you are about to make an excuse as to why you are not be able to do it, look at yourself and remind yourself that whenever you look for excuses, you will always find them; but if you don't, there is no telling to what you can achieve.

3. Readjust your mindset and how you see failure. The truth is that many people (CEOs inclusive) do not like failure. As a matter of fact, no one likes to fail. This is why when a child fails an exam, he gets sad and the people who are his sponsors get sad also. No one loves to fail.

This is the thing about failing. Successful CEOs and entrepreneurs do not see failure as failure, they see it as feedback. This change in ideology gives them the ability to take up whatever it is they see and make the most out of it. If a business venture does not go well, they examine it and draw lessons from this opportunity. They look at what could have been the problem that caused the response they got, what they can learn from it, and how they can apply this knowledge moving forward. This is the mindset of a true CEO.

Reconcile with the fact that challenges will come. It is not all going to be rosy as you journey to freedom and financial independence. You will encounter hurdles, but the mindset of a CEO is one that prepares for challenges before they come. Challenges should not hold you down, rather they should be the fodder that gives you the energy to move on and do so quickly.

4. Capable CEOs are swift to action. They do not allow issues to fester, rather they deploy all they have and all they can to make sure that problems are fixed. They know that problems do not fix themselves, so they do not behave as though all is well when all is not. They understand that ignoring a problem does not make it go away, so they face their fears head-on. This is one mindset hack you must have. Ignoring your problems does not make them go away; they only compound that way.

5. As a CEO, you need to be determined, driven, and disciplined. This is how you stay relevant and make sure that your company grows into that version of itself you have seen. If you are not driven, you will be unable to make the most out of your journey to entrepreneurship because you will not be able to control yourself and point others on the path they must follow.

Key Points From This Chapter

1. It takes more to be a successful CEO than just the beautiful and flashy things that attract your attention. If you do not know this, you will end up looking for something that you are not yet equipped to get.

2. Being a successful CEO is easier said than done. You need to be driven, and there are certain things that must happen in and to your mindset before you can be a successful CEO. Take the mind hacks that are outlined in this chapter to heart, put them to practice, and you will be amazed at what will happen.

8

RETIREMENT INVESTING FOR GENERATIONAL WEALTH

You only live once.

There is no need trying to turn deaf ears and blind eyes to this. It is the truth, and everyone knows this today. The challenge is that many people who venture into investing and business generally do not think of what and how they can create wealth in such a way that it does not end/die/finish with them. As you journey to financial freedom, at some point you must start thinking of the next generation of people coming after you, and you need to know that you can leave money for them in the form of investments.

This is part of what smart investors think – how their children and grandchildren can benefit from their wealth. More than this, they think of how younger generations can benefit from their wealth. If you are not yet thinking about this, it is time for you to start doing so.

Here are a few things you can do to set up your financial future and be sure you are safe.

1. Pay yourself first. There is no need that you go to all these lengths to get money and be paid, and you cannot take this money to treat and look after yourself with. Set up accounts that you can fall back on, in case things that are not expected should happen. Set up emergency funding for your health, career, personal ends, family, and other things in-between. Also, set up a pension fund for yourself. You do not want to retire and have your income streams dry up because you are no more actively working. If that is possible, set up a life insurance scheme with an insurance company.

2. Set up a scheme for your family and the ones you love. As you do all these for yourself, try to do the same for the people you love. Begin by getting investments for your family members, notwithstanding how little they are. Allow these to compound over time, and they will be a great source of income for them. Stocks, bonds, name them … get all of them for the people in your life, especially mem bers of your immediate family.

3. The bigger you are and the more money and assets you have, it is more advisable that you put your will together. This may sound a bit abstract because no one wants to die, and no one is saying you will. But this is life, and life is unpredictable. As much as it lies within you, get this out of the way immediately.

4. The older you and your children get, begin to teach them the rudiments of business. Do not force them because not all of them may want to go that way in life; but for those who do want to learn, teach them all you have learned, and you will be glad you did. This is one sure way to preserve the legacy you have created for yourself and make sure things do not go south even after you leave.

Remember to invest in securities for the next generation. Leave wealth and a wealth of knowledge behind for them. That way, you will give them a head start in life.

Key Points From Chapter Eight

No one wants to be reminded of the fact that sooner or later, he will be no more. As much as this is a sore subject for many people, we cannot afford to brush it under the carpet and pretend as if it is not going to happen. The steps outlined in this chapter are useful in making sure that you do not lose all you have struggled to build in a heartbeat; and it will also make sure that you give the next generation the head start they need to make their lives the best possible.

9

THE EVOLUTION OF AN INVESTOR

We all see life as a breath of fresh air, but as you grow older, you discover that it is not that easy. Life is only but a fart; and one that is smelly and stinky, if you do not prepare for it as you ought to.

For as long as I can remember, I always wanted to be financially free. Next to that, I wanted to let others perceive these wisps of fresh air which I perceived.

This implies that I wanted to show people how to get started with investing and making profits from that, and also to live the lives of their dreams. This is one thing I hope with all my heart that this book does for you – given insight on what you need to do now to start building the life you deserve for yourself.

I hope you have seen hope in the pages of this book, and you have come to be aware that financial freedom is not for a select few, but for us all.

In reading this book, you have taken the first step toward becoming all you have ever dreamed of. Now that you have the knowledge, put in the work. You can do it, and I believe in you already. Believe in yourself. Know that you have the power to be the person you want to be; the person that is not held back by financial challenges and pressure, the person that has built a Fortune 500 company who can leave a legacy for the next generation.

Can you see yourself as that person? I can. This is no ordinary pep talk. I know that if I could do it, then you can, and you will.

My final words to you are:

- get started immediately;

- pass on the knowledge from this book.

- Tell them to pass it on; and,

- We can light up this dark world to be financially free

together.

Remember, the life you desire, you deserve.

Made in the USA
Middletown, DE
26 March 2021